SECRET CHISLEHURST

Joanna Friel
& Adam Swaine

AMBERLEY

With thanks to Don, Michael and all my 'foot soldiers'.
J.F.

Photographs by Adam Swaine

First published 2015

Amberley Publishing
The Hill, Stroud
Gloucestershire, GL5 4EP

www.amberley-books.com

Copyright © Joanna Friel and Adam Swaine, 2015

The right of Joanna Friel and Adam Swaine to be
identified as the Authors of this work has been
asserted in accordance with the Copyrights, Designs
and Patents Act 1988.

ISBN 978 1 4456 4561 2 (print)
ISBN 978 1 4456 4596 8 (ebook)

British Library Cataloguing in Publication Data.
A catalogue record for this book is available from the
British Library.

Typesetting by Amberley Publishing.
Printed in Great Britain.

Contents

About the Authors

Joanna Friel studied Economic and Social History at the University of Sheffield, going on to a Postgraduate Diploma at the University of Reading. Qualified as a careers advisor, she worked with young people in south London for twenty-seven years. Following a diagnosis of multiple sclerosis in 2002 she now volunteers with The Chislehurst Society as their Heritage Representative. A resident of Chislehurst, she wrote *Chislehurst Through Time* in 2013 for Amberley Publishing. Joanna chairs The Chislehurst Society History Group, delighting in learning new information and finding old photographs which help open up the secrets of Chislehurst's past.

Adam Swaine has been a photographer for the past thirty years, covering the beautiful landscapes and villages of England and Wales. Canon is his camera of choice and his work can be seen in various magazines such as *Country Living* and *Kent Life* as well as in calendars and Tourist Board promotions. His images here unlock the secrets of Chislehurst.

Introduction

Chislehurst is a fascinating place with a rich heritage; it retains a village atmosphere despite being a suburban development in the London Borough of Bromley. Even with a wealth of source material and documented history there are always new facts to learn and pieces of jigsaw to put together. Secret Chislehurst reveals the lesser known features of this village and describes some of the different aspects of its history.

The name Chislehurst literally means a stony place in the woods. The village is surrounded by National Trust woodland, Scadbury Park and Chislehurst Commons, conserved as open space in perpetuity by Acts of Parliament. In the centre of the village the High Street was originally known as Prickend, reflecting the end of the gorse bushes on the Common.

Scadbury Manor in Chislehurst was a royal manor held by the wealthy Walsingham family from 1424; in the 1580's Sir Thomas Walsingham was a patron of playwright Christopher Marlowe. Did you realise that had a North American theatre critic proved his hypothesis, Chislehurst might well have become the new Stratford upon Avon?

Frognal, on the northern boundary of Scadbury, was home to successive Lords of the Manor, Thomas Townshend, 1st Viscount Sydney, was the first of his family to live there. He was Home Secretary under William Pitt and was responsible for the plans to send convicts to Australia. The city of Sydney, Australia is named after this illustrious resident. Do you know how many links Chislehurst has with the antipodes?

Did you know that the shutter telegraph mechanism, invented by the grandfather of the Chislehurst rector who compiled *Hymns Ancient and Modern*, was situated on high ground in Chislehurst relaying messages between London and Deal, in Kent, in fifteen minutes? Or that, tucked away in a private garden, stand two former limekilns, representing an industry once thriving in the district but long since abandoned, overtaken by the passage of time.

Significant change came to the village with the arrival of the railway in 1865. This sparked the beginning of a housing boom and the village became home to wealthy East India merchants, lawyers and bankers. Great estates flourished in the area and some vestiges remain to this day, gatehouses and laundry blocks revealing the secrets of the past.

But did you know, for example, that the founder of Great Ormond Street Hospital lies buried in the same churchyard as the one which once saw the grand funeral of the last Emperor of France? Queen Victoria visited Chislehurst on several occasions to visit the exiled French Imperial family, Emperor Louis Napoleon III, Empress Eugenie and their son the Prince Imperial. They lived at Camden Place, the former home of antiquarian William Camden. The Imperial legacy lasts to this day, with road names in their memory, telephone numbers that reflect the IMP/467 Imperial Exchange, monuments and stone eagles aloft on the chapel of St Mary's church where father and son were initially laid to rest. The quiet village of Chislehurst was momentarily the centre of European attention at the funerals of the Emperor, and that of his son some six years later.

Great mansions were built as the area became popular following the Imperial legacy and renowned architects such as E. J. May and Ernest Newton, left trademark houses which are now in the Chislehurst Conservation Area. In times of conflict these great houses played their part, being swiftly converted in hospitals during the First World War and then accommodating refugee children from war-torn Europe in 1939.

More recent times have seen new characters emerge in research; the founder of the RAC, Frederick Simms, the author of the *Just William* books, Richmal Crompton, and the creator of *Dixon of Dock Green*, Ted Willis, all lived locally.

Chislehurst is a special place of distinctive character where commuters to London also enjoy the Kent countryside, getting the best of both worlds. The village has seen change and development across the generations, but its charm remains intact to be discovered by both visitors and residents alike. Discover its secrets for yourself.

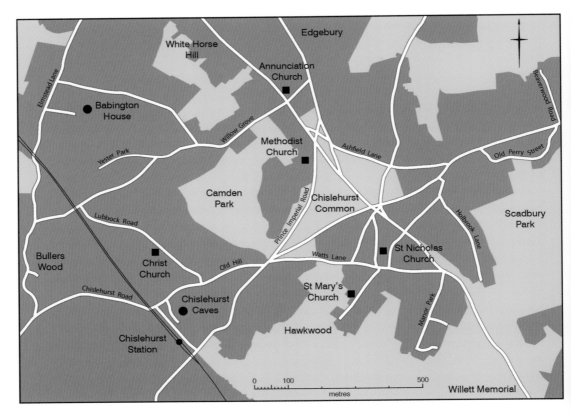

Map by Philip Sinton

1. Chequered Careers and Conundrums

DID YOU KNOW THAT...?

1. Two intriguing follies stand in Susan Wood, said to be a place where a secret subterranean garden grew.
2. A Chislehurst resident secured the presidency of Theodore Roosevelt by way of a diplomatic incident in Morocco.
3. The course of Home Rule in Ireland was forestalled by the death of a little girl buried in St Mary's Churchyard.

Follies

If you venture into Susan Wood, off Old Hill, you will come across two ornamental follies which are now Grade II-listed buildings in the grounds of Morland House. The folly to the west (*overleaf*) is one of a pair of towers created around 1860 by landowner George Baskcomb for his landscape garden, using reject Burr bricks with stone dressings from onsite works in Chislehurst Caves. It is a Gothic-style tower of two storeys, circular on the outside and octagonal to the upper floor of the interior. There are four turrets with lancet openings, conical stone caps and stepped conical pendants. The first floor has a Romanesque-style two-light window. The ground floor has lancet and two Romanesque-style arches with a clustered column. The interior is lined with 'Roman cement' but the roof and floor are missing.

The folly to the north (*overleaf*) is similar but consists of four storeys, with a circular stair turret. There are arrow slit openings on each floor. The ground floor has three round-headed openings to the main tower and one to the stair turret. The roof and floor are missing and only some of the spiral stairs remain with open treads. One is not encouraged to venture too close as the land is private.

George Baskcomb was the grandson of the parish clerk of St Nicholas church. He lived at the so called 'Manor House' and was at one time owner of the windmill on the Common which had provided a share of its flour on Mondays and Tuesdays to the needy. The mill was in disrepair when Baskcomb and other shareholders acquired it in 1868; Baskcomb bought the others out and pulled the mill down in 1876. Mill Place just above Susan Wood and the Imperial Arms public house (which was originally called The Windmill) are both reminders of the corn grinding era.

Susan Wood was once called Denbridge Wood, part of the larger Chalkpit Wood. Who 'Susan' was has never been discovered – Baskcomb's wife was called Sarah – the secret

Susan Woods limekilns.

Left and below right: West folly.

Below left: North folly.

probably lies with George, who in later life lived in a house called Summerhill where he developed his landscape garden over Chalkpit Wood. According to *The History of Chislehurst*:

> Denbridge Wood terminates at a cliff formed by a chalk quarry of large extent. Its bed is about twenty feet below the surface and it contains about three acres of land. The chalk workings penetrate far under the hill, forming a long series of galleries about twelve feet in height. The entrances to the quarry are blocked up (1899) but Mr Baskcomb was able to enter from his garden, by a funnel-shaped descent terminating in a staircase. He used to spend a good deal of his time in them, and had formed a subterranean kitchen garden, where he used to grow celery and other vegetables. They contain a very deep well of pure water.

It is likely that these follies are actually old limekilns from the days of lime burning from chalk for both mortar construction and agricultural fertiliser. Baskcomb converted them into follies and today they are covered in ivy and surrounded by trees but magnificent reminders of their industrial past.

The Perdicaris Affair

A diplomatic incident involving a Chislehurst resident, US President Theodore Roosevelt and a Moroccan outlaw.

Ion Perdicaris, a resident of the Manor House in 1911, was a key character in the re-election of President Theodore Roosevelt yet his name is largely unknown.

Ion's father was a former Consul from Greece and a successful businessman. His mother was the daughter of a wealthy South Carolinian family. Ion maintained a playboy lifestyle until the American Civil War began to threaten his fortune. Fearing confiscation of his holdings, he travelled to Greece and abandoned his American citizenship. He eventually moved to Tangier in Morocco, built a house he called 'The Place of Nightingales' and filled it with exotic animals.

While on a visit to England, Perdicaris met Ellen Varley, the wife of a well known transatlantic cable engineer. They began an affair and two years later Ellen, now divorced, joined Perdicaris in Tangier, bringing her children with her.

Life came to an abrupt halt in May 1904 when Ellen's son, Cromwell Varley, and Ion were kidnapped by a tribal pretender to the throne of Morocco, Mulai Amhed er Raisuli, known as the 'Last of the Barbary Pirates'. The ransom demanded of the Sultan of Morocco was $70,000 and control of two of the wealthiest districts of the country.

Back in the US, word that a prominent American citizen (or so it was thought) had been abducted, outraged President Roosevelt, who immediately ordered seven warships to secure the abductees and protect Mrs Perdicaris, as Ellen had now become. Roosevelt unsuccessfully attempted to persuade Britain and France to join him in this endeavour. The American Secretary of State declared that 'this government wants Perdicaris alive or Raisuli dead'. By 21 June 1904, the Sultan agreed to meet Raisuli's demands and Roosevelt emerged as a hero in the eyes of Americans: courageous in the defence of Americans anywhere on the globe. Roosevelt won a landslide election victory that year!

Ion, Ellen and the family moved back to England and settled in Chislehurst, the 1911 census has the whole family and servants in situ at the Manor House. Ellen died in 1920 and Ion in 1925. They are both buried in St Nicholas churchyard where the tombstone clearly shows his abodes as Trenton, New Jersey, Tangier and Chislehurst. However, the revelation that he was no longer an American citizen at the time of the incident remained a secret until 1933, though by then the reaction was muted.

Grave of Ion Perdicaris.

The Cockpit

This circular depression on the common to the west of St Nicholas church is known as The Cockpit and is believed to be the only known remaining example of its kind in the country. It was used for cockfighting and singlestick play, or cudgels – the use of a wooden stick as a way of training soldiers in swordsmanship. It is probably a former gravel pit and was adapted for use as a cockpit. It is now 1.5 metres deep, 38 metres in diameter and has gently sloping sides. On the floor of the pit there is an inner-circular enclosure, 11 metres in diameter surrounded by a raised path and on the west side a path leads down to the inner enclosure.

Cockfighting was abolished by Act of Parliament in 1834 but singlestick went on until 1862 when it too was abolished because it had become 'the resort of all the commonest and lowest class of persons'.

The Cockpit has long been a place of assembly for the village. In 1814 people gathered for tea in celebration of the Treaty of Paris and what was thought to be the end of Napoleon Bonaparte – how bizarre that his nephew should live just a few hundred yards away some decades later. In 1919, the Cockpit was the gathering place for a special service of thanksgiving for the returning soldiers at the end of the Great War.

The stone marker on the edge of the slope was the gift of Chislehurst resident, Mr A. L. Gunn.

Stone marker.

A Whale of a Story

In *Imperial Chislehurst* T. A. Bushell writes about 'lost' roads. Many of these remain a secret, but curiously one of these relates to a whale bone which can be found on Chislehurst Common.

The lost road in question is the one that continued from Heathfield Lane, through the common, to St Nicholas School. Running below this lost road is the water course that drains the Overflow Pond (an almost secret everglade in itself) and on its way to Rush Pond it goes under the wide path on the east side of the main road. This was once the starting point of a racecourse. The horses did a U-turn above Prickend Pond (named after the prickly gorse on the Common) and then ran south on the other side of the main road.

The crossing on Bromley Road was marked by two posts made of whalebone and the finish at the gates of Camden Court (now Camden Close) by two more. There is also said to have been a whalebone arch at one time within the grounds of what was then Canister House, which became Camden Court, placed there by the owner Admiral Wells or another member of the family. Admiral Wells sold Canister House to his brother, who then leased it to Captain Edwards, formerly of the navy – perhaps he went whaling in his time at sea!

During the Napoleonic Wars at the beginning of the1800s, part of the course, the home straight, was cultivated to grow potatoes by the inhabitants of the poor house. This part

Whale bone.

was more or less opposite the present Methodist church on Prince Imperial Road. Racing ceased about 1870, around the time that housing was being developed in the area.

The only surviving remnant of whale bone is at the finish line near the entrance to Camden Close. Take a careful look; it is similar to a tree stump. The Commons Trustees take great care to see that it is not 'chopped' down.

The Irish Question

An illegitimate baby for Kitty O'Shea

A baby girl by the name of Claude Sophie, who died aged two months, is buried in St Mary's Roman Catholic churchyard. Was her birth as an illegitimate child, and the resulting scandal, a significant turning point in Irish politics in the nineteenth century, leading to the downfall of Charles Stewart Parnell?

The girl's mother was Katherine O'Shea; her father was Parnell, the leader of the Irish Parliamentary Party at a time when Irish Home Rule was a major political issue.

Katherine O'Shea was of aristocratic stock, born in Essex in 1846, the daughter of Sir John Page Wood and the granddaughter of a former Lord Mayor of London. Her friends

Grave of Claude Sophie O'Shea.

called her Katie, her enemies 'Kitty', (a slang term for a prostitute). She had married Captain William O'Shea, a Catholic Nationalist MP but was already separated from him in 1880 when she met Parnell. Her family had connections to the Liberal Party and she acted as go-between with Parnell and Prime Minister William Gladstone during negotiations to introduce the first Irish Home Rule Bill in 1886.

As leader of his party, Parnell had toured America in 1879 to raise funds for famine relief in Ireland and also to secure support for Home Rule; he was dubbed 'the uncrowned King of Ireland'. Parnell, an Anglican, knew that the explicit endorsement of Catholic Church leaders in Ireland was of vital importance to his success, and he worked particularly closely with them to consolidate their hold over the Irish electorate. His party is generally seen as the first modern British political party, with an efficient structure and control by the leadership, and by 1885 he was leading a party destined to secure Home Rule for Ireland.

Gladstone described Parnell as one of the most remarkable people he had ever met. Parnell worked carefully towards the details of a Home Rule Bill with Gladstone. However, disaster struck when William O'Shea filed for divorce citing Parnell as co-respondent.

Parnell had moved into Katie's home in nearby Eltham; they were to have three children together, all out of wedlock, the first being Claude Sophie. Captain O'Shea knew about the relationship, he challenged Parnell to a duel and forbade his wife from seeing Parnell, although she claimed that he had encouraged her in the relationship. O'Shea eventually filed for divorce in 1889 (following the death of Katie's aunt and an expected legacy being held in trust but not passed to him). Parnell's relationship with Katie had been the subject of gossip in London political circles for many years but, with the scandal of the divorce and their adultery, this was further sensationalised when the custody of her two remaining daughters by Parnell was awarded to Captain O'Shea.

After the divorce, Parnell married Katie but he had been deserted by the majority of his own Irish Parliamentary Party resulting in his downfall as its leader in December 1890. His career ruined and his health shattered by the crisis, he died aged only forty-five in the arms of his wife, less than four months after their marriage. The cause was cancer of the stomach, possibly complicated by coronary heart disease. Katie lived the rest of her life in relative obscurity in Sussex until her death in 1921 aged seventy-five.

Historians ponder if, had Parnell lived, Irish Home Rule could have happened earlier but his involvement in the O'Shea divorce changed the shape of late nineteenth-century politics to an extent that can only be speculated upon. He had been prepared to sacrifice everything for his love of Mrs O'Shea, a love that was first demonstrated by the birth of little Claude Sophie. Despite the fact that her parents were not married at the time and that her father was an Anglican, she was laid to rest in the nearest Catholic burial ground to Eltham, namely, St Mary's, Chislehurst.

An important moment in Anglo-Irish relations; not so much a secret, more a tragic representation of a lost political career.

St Aidan's Church, Edgebury

On the very northern boundary of Chislehurst, on Imperial Way, there is still a signpost pointing to St Aiden's, a church that no longer exists!

The church of St Aiden's was in Gravelwood Close and was built in 1957 having been commissioned by the Rochester Diocese and was paid for with money given by the government for the rebuilding of war-damaged All Hallows Church, Southwark. Strangely, St Aidan's was a subsidiary church of All Saints, New Eltham and designed to be a mission church. As well as a church, it was to be a community centre with seats for 100 people. It was simply built with brick cavity walls, tubular steel columns and a single chiming bell. It was the shortest-lived church in Chislehurst; closing in December 1974.

The building was sold in 1977 to the Scouts and was still used by the community until 1994. The site was eventually sold in 2001 and the church building was demolished for housing.

Many people remember singing in the choir there or being altar boys as well as it being an active youth club. If the sign had been removed we then might not have known to investigate further. Happy memories for many have been stirred up on Facebook.

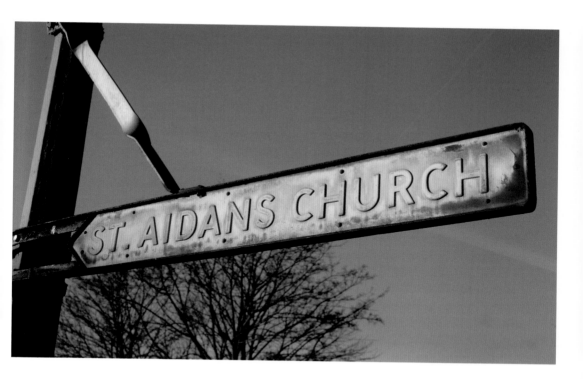

2. Curiosities

Telegraph Path

What is the secret of this unremarkable footpath leading across the brow of the hill from White Horse Hill to Green Lane? The name harks back to the Napoleonic Wars when Chislehurst played a significant part in relaying messages from London to the south coast. The shutter telegraph system was invented by Lord George Murray. He became the bishop of St David's in Wales and was also the grandfather of the most renowned nineteenth-century rector of St Nicholas church in Chislehurst, Canon Francis Murray.

In the 1790s, the French had developed a system of visual communication using signals and England was on high alert recognising the need to be prepared for the threat of invasion should it come. The French were using a T – Telegraph System which conveyed 9,999 separate words, all listed in a code book.

Murray's British system was ingenious in its simplicity. It could convey words, letter by letter, by means of six moveable shutters on a frame. Six shutters could be arranged in sixty-four different ways so there was scope to include useful phrases and numbers. The codes became public knowledge and could be read by anyone interested. Murray was awarded £2,000 for his shutter telegraph which was used across the south of England. The shutters were placed on the roofs of specially constructed cottages which were built at intervals on high ground, within eyesight, between London and the south coast between Portsmouth and Deal.

The Chislehurst shutter telegraph was erected in 1796 on the west side of Green Lane, communicating with Forest Hill and Birchwood Corner, Swanley and so on to Chatham. At this point the land is 90 metres above sea level, though at the time of the shutter telegraph it would have been even higher; the road summit has been twice lowered in the nineteenth century to make it easier for traffic. Telegraph Hill in New Cross gets its name from the same system on the route. On plotting the route, it is quite remarkable how

straight the lines are across the hill tops turning at Chislehurst. A message could have been relayed between London and the south coast in fifteen minutes.

Of course it was all dependent on the weather and the time of day. There is no denying that on a clear day the current view from Telegraph Path towards Canary Wharf is stunning, giving a real sense of height. An obvious place to put the shutter telegraph.

Royal Parade Letter Box

The attractive hexagonal pillar box at the north-end of Royal Parade holds a secret. This 'Penfold' design letter box may look like 'the real deal', of the type constructed in the late 1870s but it is merely a pastiche put there in 1990 to enhance the streetscape in line with the grand title of the parade of shops.

Cow Path

There is a path which connects the Chislehurst Recreation Ground to Elmstead Lane, known locally as the Cow Path. It once had open meadows on either side, and in the late 1800s farmers used this path to herd their cows from the farms at Elmstead Lane up and into the village.

Cow path.

The agricultural past of the village can be unearthed from articles in the local paper, *The Chislehurst Times*. A former resident wrote about his memories of seeing prisoners of war being taken to the fields beyond Green Lane to pick asparagus and Victoria Road was nicknamed Cabbage Alley as there were cabbage fields at the end of the road.

To the south of the Cow Path was a large rambling mansion named Waratah on Waldon Road, built around 1893. The Holt family were resident there at the time and William Lund, owner of the Blue Anchor Shipping Line had as his flagship, SS *Waratah*. The ship went down in 1909 with the loss of all on board. Waratah is today the emblem of New South Wales, Australia.

The mansion was occupied until 1940 when it was used as storage for Harrison Gibsons furniture retailers of Bromley. On 4 February 1944 the mansion was hit by an incendiary bomb and seriously damaged by fire; it was demolished in the early 1960s. Ravensbourne College of Art and Design was built on the site in the mid-seventies and was the site of an early performance by the Sex Pistols. The college moved to the O2 Arena and the land was developed for housing known as King's Quarter.

St Michael's Orphanage

Above: St Michael's orphanage.

Right: Manning and Anderdon Almshouses

This large building was the original poorhouse of 1759 where paupers were given work. From 1861 it became an orphanage and subsequently a children's home. The two outer gabled wings are the remnants of the original building and the projecting central gable was added in 1862, a later Arts and Crafts addition is *c.* 1885.

St Michael's Orphanage was run by Anne and Maria Anderdon, sisters in law of Canon Francis Murray of St Nicholas church. These philanthropic sisters also founded the almshouses off the High Street in 1881. Their uncle was Cardinal Manning, archbishop of Westminster Cathedral, hence the name Manning and Anderdon Almshouses. Cardinal Manning was also related by marriage to local resident Henry Clutton, the architect of St Mary's Roman Catholic chapel; Manning is believed to have played cricket here in Chislehurst.

The Governesses' Institute

Governesses' Institute plaque.

While on the subject of benevolence, it is worth remembering the innocuous building dating back to 1975 that was Queen Mary's House. In 1871 the original building was known as the Governesses' Institute – The Asylum for Aged Governesses, designed by Thomas H. Wyatt. There was a brass foundation plaque from the original building inside the entrance. Canon Murray, the proponent of the book *The History of Chislehurst* was present at the first building's opening. At the time of publication the residential home has closed but the charitable foundation remains in operation. This plaque has been donated to the Chislehurst Society.

Guiding

A more modern dedication plaque can be seen, if you know where to look, at Christ Church, commemorating the planting of a beech hedge in the church grounds to celebrate fifty years of Girl Guiding locally. The plaque is embedded in the wooden handrail at the far steps leading to the church centre.

Guiding Plaque at Christ Church.

St Nicholas Church

The little window revealed in 1957 during exploratory works to the west flank of St Nicholas church may have revealed the secret of the church's age. It is thought that this window is original, what we see represents the whole window, very small, and typical of its kind.

The church architect considered it to 'be of early Norman or Saxon date'. It has been described as belonging to a class of primitive windows or loops, found in a number of churches in Kent. They are generally accepted as pre Norman Conquest in age.

The internal workings of the church clock are hidden from the senses, and are a horological gem. The clock was installed, along with the eight bells in 1857, with a plate by the manufacturer, F. Dent, dated 1858.

It is similar to that in the clock tower of the Palace of Westminster (think Big Ben) and has the same mechanism, known as an 'escapement'. This device aims to isolate the movement of the clock pendulum from the clock gearing to achieve great accuracy. It is known as a three-legged double escapement and is, possibly, a prototype for the clock at the Houses of Parliament. It is a complex devise; for an insight into the Grimthorpe escapement one is best advised to go to www.trin.can.ac.uk/clock/escapement or, better still, climb the clock tower on open days and see it for yourself.

St Nicholas' church and clock.

There is, however, one further little secret yet to be resolved regarding the church bells. Mr Denison, later Lord Grimthorpe, acted as 'bell adviser' to Revd Wollaston's 1857 Tower Committee. The reverend is quoted as saying 'If you insist on the installation of eight bells, I shall have no further involvement with the project. There is insufficient room in the tower'. There are eight bells to this day so space must have been found, with or without the reverend's input!

St Nicholas' church bell.

The Millennium Rock

The granite boulder on the Common, opposite Hornbrook car park, is over two billion years old. Bromley Council purchased several of these rocks and had them placed in different parts of the borough as part of the millennium celebrations. The rocks are Lewisian Gneiss (metamorphic rock stretching from Lewis in the Outer Hebrides to the mainland) from Lochinver in North West Scotland, one of the oldest rocks seams in the British Isles.

This particular boulder did not get its plaque until 2007 when Chislehurst Rotary Club organised the dedication and 'unveiling'; the plaque can be seen from the Common not the main road.

Millennium rock.

Bullers Wood, Ernest Newton and William Morris

Ernest Newton was a founder member of the Art Workers Guild in the 1880s and associated with the leading figures of the Arts and Crafts Movement of that time. He developed a career designing one-off houses largely in Bromley and Bickley and later concentrated on country house commissions. In the 1890s he acted as consultant architect to William Willett, the Chislehurst developer who is considered to be the instigator of British Summer Time.

One of Newton's local works was the remodelling of Bullers Wood House for its owners, the Sanderson family. The school, as it is today, owns a signed book of his plans and drawings. The attractive gate, which is an entrance to the grounds, marks the date of the changes, 1890 (overleaf).

William Morris was commissioned by Newton to design some of the interior redecoration including the stunning stencilled ceiling in the library that can still be seen on open days. Bullers Wood was Morris's last residential commission and a letter written by his wife, Jane, commenting after a visit to Chislehurst, makes interesting reading: 'Villas, nothing but villas, save a chemist's shop and a dry public house near the station: no sign of any common people, or anything but gentlemen and servants – a beastly place to live in, don't you think?'

Bullers Wood gate.

Western Motor Works

Hugh Marsham-Townshend, a descendant of the Sydney family, received a wedding gift from his father in 1904, a 15 H. P. Panhard Levassor car supplied by C. S. Rolls & Co. of West Brompton; Rolls was Hugh's cousin.

Hugh's younger brother, Ferdinand was particularly enthusiastic about motoring and set up a motorcar business in the stables of the family home at Frognal (in what is now Sidcup). He had wanted to have his business in Knightsbridge and to call it West End Motor Works. However, failing to find suitable premises, he merely adapted the name to become Western Motor Works.

In 1905 he recruited H. C. Bennett from Rolls with a team of staff. Soon the Frognal business was flourishing and new premises were required to cope with the volume of work. In 1909 the new building on Perry Street became the first purpose-built motor car service station in the country.

The robust construction of the building was designed by local architect E. J. May. There was an inspection pit, and a gas engine provided the power. The workshop was illuminated by state of the art Blanchard paraffin-burning incandescent lamps. The overall cost of the build was £1,443 7s 2d with a further £183 5s 4d for the office. Everything was ready for the first vehicle, but its roof was torn off on arrival because the entrance door was too low. There were already 17,860 cars on the road, a number that increased to 100,000 by 1914. The machine shop was by then a hive of activity; its equipment was found to be ideal for the making of shell caps and production mounted to thousands upon thousands during the First World War.

Western Motor Works by E. J. May.

The war was to claim the life of Ferdinand; he was killed in action in May 1915. His memorial is in the Scadbury Chapel at St Nicholas church. The business passed to his brother, Hugh, and in 1920 he passed the ownership to H. C. Bennett.

Bennett expanded the business and weathered the difficult period in the 1920s. He became an Austin main agent in 1923 and a distributor of the Chevrolet, a General Motors product. In 1928 Vauxhall came under the control of General Motors and Western Motor works began their long association with GM in 1933.

During the Second World War the firm was reconditioning bomb damaged machinery and making detonator mechanisms for underwater mines.

But what became of the car that started it all? Before he died In July 1954 H.C. Bennett wrote to Hugh Marsham-Townshend asking if he could purchase for the firm the old red Panhard. It was still going strong, having been used for the delivery of the mail in 1926 during the General Strike and it had been continually serviced at Perry Street. Hugh insisted that Bennett should have it as a present, and although sometimes referred to as The Old Lady, it stood for many years in place of honour in the Perry Street showroom.

The car is now a member of the Veteran Car Club and competes in the London to Brighton Rally.

Elmstead Woods Station Garden

Elmstead station was opened 1 July 1904, after rebuilding the collapsed northern railway tunnel in 1903. Tunnels were demanded by the landowners of Sundridge Park, the Scotts, who refused access to their land during construction. 'Woods' was added to the station name 1 October 1908.

Elmstead Woods
Station Garden.

The name is particularly charming given that the station is possibly one of the most attractive on the line with its flourishing 'garden'. The gardens stretch the length of the 300 metre long platforms.

The instigator of the garden was Kenneth Bilbrough from Elmstead Grange (now Babington House School). In 1905 he extended his hobby of gardening to include creating the gardens at the station. He tended these for thirty years and it is his legacy that continues for commuters to appreciate today.

In August 1995 *Daily Mail* published an article titled 'The Garden now Standing on Platform Three' about Elmstead Woods Station. The article featured the work of Howard

Pettit and Peter Phelps who gardened at the station in the late 1980s. The station had been extended at that time and in the course of clearing up the mess a pond was created in the hole left after the diesel-contaminated soil was removed. Unwanted cobblestones from another station became the foundations for the rockery.

Today there is an enthusiastic gardening club meeting every few weeks and new volunteers are always welcome. The club has been supported by The Chislehurst Society, commercial sponsors and the railway company.

Inaccessible to the public is Elmstead Pit, outside the station, a Site of Special Scientific Interest formerly known as Rock Pits. The pit exposes an important layer of Oldhaven or Blackheath Beds laid down over 50 million years ago and on which much of Chislehurst lies. Fossils including sharks teeth, fish scales and molluscs demonstrate the sub-tidal estuary environment that once existed here.

Methodist Church

Built in the early English Gothic Style, Chislehurst Methodist Church was opened in 1870 as the Wesleyan Chapel. It was built on the edge of the common, on what is now Prince Imperial Road, with funds donated from local residents, George Hayter Chubb and brothers, James and William Vanner. James was Sunday School Superintendent and William was the organist for thirty years. All three are commemorated by tablets on the wall of the nave. The plaques can be seen on the opposite page.

The Damascene Labyrinth

A glass canopy connects the church with its hall and the resulting community space is enjoyed by many local groups. Perhaps the most remarkable feature is the labyrinth design set in a new tiled floor surface in the main body of the church (pictured overleaf). This stunning pattern is often secret because the building is in constant use but on rare days of inactivity it is revealed.

The designer, Jeff Saward, took his inspiration from a water labyrinth in the Qasr al-Azm Palace in Damascus, Syria which dates from around 1750. In common with the original this maze-like labyrinth features separate paths for inward and outward spiritual journeys.

The Church Organ and the Curious Story of George Watto, c. 1844–1931

The grade II-listed organ built by Forster and Andrews of Hull was installed in 1883. It has 1,600 pipes, many of them ornately painted. Originally it was pumped by hand bellows but today it is electrically operated. The organs are pictured overleaf.

George Watto of Willow Grove provided the man power for the bellows for many years. Watto came from the Africa, allegedly rescued from a group of Portuguese slave traders by Dr David Livingstone. He claimed he was one of six boys who brought Dr Livingstone's body home to England and in the book *Black Londoners* by Susan Okokan the author said, 'Watto came to London in 1886 as one of the bearers of Dr Livingstone's coffin.'

Two plaques from the Methodist church.

Above: Damascene Labyrinth. *Below:* Methodist church organ pipes.

However, further research has shown that there is no evidence of any connection between George Watto and David Livingstone. The truth is that the only black coffin bearer was a man called Jacob Wainwright and furthermore Livingstone's funeral took place in 1874 after his death in what is now Zambia in May 1873 from malaria.

George Watto was something of a character. On official documents, his name is variously spelt Watto, Wattow, Whottow and Watteau. The Watteau spelling gave rise to the story that he married a French servant from the household of the Empress Eugenie, and assumed his supposed wife's name. In fact, he married a local girl, Martha Holmes, a laundress.

He worked as a gardener for the Vanners, who lived at Camden Wood, then called Beechcroft and now called Livingstone House (perhaps inspired by this curious tale?). Watto was regarded with some trepidation by children, whom he would chase with his spear in jest.

Watto was allegedly sacked from his job pumping the bellows for the organ because of his habit of peering over the organ screen during sermons and confronting members of the congregation with grimaces, before disappearing from view again. His name probably came from his habitual greeting of 'What Ho!' and, as he was illiterate, its many spellings are understandable.

He died in 1931, aged about eighty-seven. The local paper published a photo of him holding a spear, standing by a picture of Livingstone, saying he was the last survivor of the expedition.

George Watto, the slave rescued by Dr Livingstone, who found a new home in Kent

Slave saved by Victorian explorer

(LATE NOV 2006)

The church displays a different newspaper article about him.

3. Connections with Australia

The Sydney Connection

When the Hon. Thomas Townshend died in 1780 he was succeeded by his son, Thomas. The family home was Frognal, (now in Sidcup, but at that time part of Chislehurst) their previous home, the moated manor of Scadbury, having been abandoned in 1752. Thomas, like his father and grandfather, entered politics, as MP for Whitchurch, a seat which he held for twenty-nine years until 1783, when he was created Baron Sydney, and entered the House of Lords.

He originally proposed the title Baron Sidney, (spelt with an 'i' not with a 'y') in honour of a distant family member, Algernon Sidney. He was worried that other members of the Sidney family wanted to use that spelling of the name. He considered Sydenham, the name of a village nearby, before deciding on Sydney.

He was an influential politician during the turbulent years of the US War of Independence and the Napoleonic Wars, holding a number of important positions, including Secretary at War, Leader of the House of Commons, Home Secretary and Leader of the House of Lords. While Home Secretary, following the loss of the colonies in the United States, Townshend was responsible for plans to send the First Fleet to Australia in 1787. He appointed Arthur Phillip as Governor of the colony, who, after Townshend had been elevated to the peerage,

Right: Sydney memorial in St Nicholas' church

Below: Lady Sydney's School, Old Perry Street.

honoured his patron by naming Sydney Cove after him. The settlement, and now the city, of Sydney, took its name from the cove. (Sydney, Nova Scotia, Canada is also named after him). In the Scadbury Chapel at St Nicholas church, is the white marble Sydney monument which is a family history lesson in itself (shown opposite).

Lady Sydney's School

The monogram of Lady Emily Sydney, the wife of the first Earl Sydney who was the grandson of the first baron, can be seen above a doorway (shown opposite) on what is now a timber merchants in Old Perry Street. School House, to the east, is so named after the school Lady Sydney founded in 1875; it became the schoolmaster's house when a new school was added to the west in 1879. The school building became a laundry in 1902 and an unusual metamorphosis to a banana importing company before its current owners took occupation.

The Sydney Arms public house (shown on opposite page), originally called The Swan, also commemorates the Sydneys of Frognal. The first evidence of its revised name is found in the Marsham-Townshend papers of 1859.

Foundation Stone at Christ Church

There is a dedication stone at Christ Church in Lubbock Road recalling its foundation on 10 June 1871 (opposite). On close inspection, one can read that Viscount Sydney laid the first stone, in fact, his wife, Lady Emily, was supposed to do the job but she was unwell on the day.

Farringtons Chapel

The magnificent bronze doors of Farringtons School chapel (overleaf) were cast in the Chubb works in Sydney and brought back to Chislehurst to fit exactly in place. Lord Hayter Chubb, of locksmith fame, (and a founder of Chislehurst Methodist Church) was a Chislehurst resident and first Chairman of this school.

Antipodean References

You can walk along Kangaroo Walk above Raggleswood, off Old Hill, though why it takes that name remains an undiscovered secret! It works both ways, there are roads in Western Australia with Chislehurst references and a women's college called Chislehurst.

An organ works (which no longer exists) off Old Hill was the place of manufacture of an organ that was destined to play in St Andrew's Cathedral in Sydney. Unfortunately the organ didn't withstand the change in climate from Chislehurst and none of it remains in place.

Botany Bay

You can also walk down Botany Bay Lane from Coopers School to Tongs Farm on the National Trust managed estate of Hawkwood. We have no proof that Botany Bay's name

Above: The Sydney Arms public house.

Right: Christ Church foundation stone.

Left: Chapel doors at Farringtons School, made in Australia.

comes from any Australian connection and it's not entirely unlikely that the name actually relates to our rich natural history.

Chislehurst's history documents several botanical specialists – George Buchanan Wollaston, architect and keen naturalist, owned Bishops Well on the Common; he was a distinguished botanist, cataloguing orchids and ferns, many now extinct, and was known as an authority on these species. He was also a friend of the Empress Eugenie, hosting a gathering at Bishops Well on the anniversary of the death of the Prince Imperial.

Sir John Lubbock, Chislehurst resident from 1861–65 and visited here by Charles Darwin on 15 February 1862, had a lifelong interest in hymenoptera (the third largest order of insects), and wrote *Ants, Wasps and Bees*, a bestseller some years after his departure from Chislehurst.

Sir John Bennett, noted clock and watchmaker, lived at Glen Druid on Yester Road. He was the grandfather of Theodore Dru Alison Cockerell, a botanist who explored, collected and published about the fauna of Chislehurst and later studied in Colorado. Cockerell is known to have stayed in Chislehurst in his youth.

John Patrick Micklethwait Brenan was born at Fairholm, Willow Grove, in 1917; he became director of the Royal Botanic Gardens at Kew.

Plant discoveries continue as a Star of Bethlehem flower has been seen growing on the commons.

4. Chislehurst Chillers

DID YOU KNOW THAT...?

1. There is a busy local junction named after a gibbet.
2. The gardeners shed in St Nicholas' churchyard has a more macabre history.
3. There are two double murders commemorated in St Nicholas' churchyard.

Hangman's Corner

At the junction of Bromley Road and Watts Lane there is a horse chestnut tree. Arthur Battle, in his book *Edwardian Chislehurst*, noted that this tree failed to thrive. Even today the tree is not tall and has consistently failed to produce a good display of bloom.

The junction is known as 'Hangman's Corner' and a stone has been placed at the base of the tree to mark the site of the gibbet. It was probably just a warning to would be felons as there is no evidence of any hangings taking place there.

There was also a small prison or lock-up in Chislehurst, known first as the watch-house and finally as the cage. It was built in 1788 on 'account of the great increase in vagrancy'. It was on the green opposite what is now Royal Parade and was a small brick building made up of two rooms, only one of which had a roof. The only bedding was a little straw on the ground. The village stocks were alongside, but these were removed after the Police Act of 1839. The cage was removed by order of the parish council in 1854.

The Mortuary Shed

In the late 1800s public houses were the only possible places to temporarily house the bodies of vagrants who did not survive the cold. Landlords naturally found this extremely disagreeable, particularly where a body was in no fit state to be brought inside. The matter was brought to a head when one local landlord refused to store a body before an inquest could be held.

A suitable building was required and part of St Nicholas' churchyard was deemed the place for the necessary mortuary shed. It was built there at the expense of the parish in 1890.

Today the shed still stands in the churchyard, its wooden cladding recently restored, funded by a grant from The Chislehurst Society. Thankfully it no longer fulfils its original function and it is used to store gardening and maintenance equipment.

Right: Hangman's Corner.

Below: The mortuary shed.

1813: Murder Most Foul

Mr and Mrs Bonar were murdered in their beds on Sunday 31 May 1813. Thomson Bonar was a wealthy merchant. He had married his younger first cousin, Anne, and they came to live at Camden Place in 1805. Despite the eleven-year age gap they were a devoted couple and often expressed the wish that, when the time came, they wanted to leave the world together. Little did they know that the grim reaper would indeed do just that.

The inquest report at the time provides a detailed report:

The seventy-year-old Mr Bonar went to bed around midnight and his wife followed him as usual at about 2.00 a.m. When Charles King, a local labourer, arrived for work at 5.30 a.m he noticed the front door was open and went to tell the footman, Philip Nicholson, the only male servant who slept in the house. The housemaid had noticed that the front door was half open and also found a window open in the drawing room. Upstairs she found the Bonar's dressing room door locked with the key on the outside. The servants went in, turned towards the beds and screamed. Both the Bonars had suffered repeated heavy blows to the head. Mr Bonar, horribly disfigured, lay in a pool of blood on the

Above: Camden Place.

floor. Mrs Bonar was still in bed. A bent bloodstained poker was found lying on the bedroom floor.

Nicholson covered Mr Bonar's body with a blanket but as he bent over Mrs Bonar he realised she was still breathing. He stripped the bloodied sheets from Mr Bonar's bed and used them to clean up the mess on the floor; he then went downstairs, still holding the bloodied sheets. Getting a sheet from his own bed, he used it to wrap the stained linen.

Nicholson insisted on going to London to fetch the noted surgeon Mr Astley Cooper to attend to Mrs Bonar. Nicholson took the best horse and set off at speed, he stopped en route three times for a glass of rum, then, after notifying, the doctor, he rode away.

Mr Cooper reached Mrs Bonar but she passed away at 1.00 p.m. Nicholson had also taken it upon himself to inform Bow Street police of the murder. At Camden Place they found a pair of bloodstained shoes by Nicholson's bed which matched footmarks on the stairs.

A warrant for Nicholson's arrest was issued and he was eventually tracked down drinking at the Three Nuns Inn, Whitechapel. He denied having heard anything in the night and said he had just used his sheets to prevent further mess. He was stripped and searched to find any bruises which might have indicated signs of a struggle. There was a clear mark sustained on his forehead.

Nicholson was taken to Camden Place to give evidence. He was locked in the butler's pantry pending questioning. It transpired that he had only been in the Bonar's employ for three weeks prior to the murder. Under questioning, he admitted that the shoes were his but thought the blood had come from the bedroom when he encountered the deceased.

As the inquest was drawing to a close Nicholson asked if he could relieve himself. He took a razor from his pocket and slit his throat. [The razor had come from the butler's pantry] The doctors attending the inquest treated him and during that time the jury returned a verdict of wilful murder.

By Wednesday evening Nicholson was able to speak, merely protesting his innocence. His demeanour was so calm it was suspected that he might try a further attempt on his own life, so he was placed in a straitjacket. In the morning Nicholson asked to see Mr Bonar junior. Nicholson burst into tears and made a full confession. Nicholson said he had neither motive nor ill will towards his employers.

The trial was held at Maidstone Assizes on 20 August, the character witness for Nicholson revealed he had previously been dismissed for drunkenness. Nicholson read a letter to the court which attributed the murder to 'a temporary fury from excessive drinking'.

Nicholson was hanged at Penenden Heath in the presence of Thomson Bonar junior.

This terrible event has been commemorated with a fulsome epitaph on the tombstone of the victims, which was quoted by Gladstone in a speech in the House of Commons following a visit to Chislehurst in 1864.Bonar Place on the edge of the former Camden Place Estate recalls the name of the tragic couple.

Left: The grave of Mr and Mrs Thomson Bonar.

31 October 1880: Felled by the Hands of an Assassin

Sadly, there is a second tomb in St Nicholas churchyard representing another murder of a husband and wife. What became known as 'The Dreadful Double Murder' of Mr and Mrs Ellis shocked the Chislehurst community. Reporting at the time made it quite a sensation, the mood being captured by the words on the grave of the victims: 'In affectionate remembrance of Edward and Elizabeth Ellis who died by the hand of an assassin.' Chillingly, the murder occurred on Halloween.

The bodies of this elderly couple were found in Petts Wood by the police, in a badly beaten state. They had been directed there by apprehended prisoner Joseph Waller. Waller had been arrested at four o'clock on Sunday morning for being in the pig sty for unlawful purposes, he was sober and calm. At the police station Waller showed his hands and said, 'There is human blood', requesting that constables be sent into the wood with stretchers to find the bodies. Six policemen found the bodies, still warm, having been shot with a revolver.

The inquest was held at The Bull. Mr Ellis, aged seventy-four, had been game-keeper to Mr Berens in Petts Wood for fifty years. Joseph Waller, aged twenty-four, had been, until recently, an assistant keeper to Mr Elllis and he made a full confession. He had been wandering for three or four hours after leaving The Five Bells in St Mary Cray at midnight with a loaded revolver in his pocket. He said he was tempted, by an uncontrollable impulse to do some 'desperate deed' and he fired off a shot in the wood behind Keepers Cottage and then called Mr Ellis saying he had seen poachers.

Ellis took his truncheon and went with Waller into the wood. About a quarter of a mile into the wood Waller shot Mr Ellis in the head and beat him with the old man's truncheon. From there Waller took Mr Ellis's now broken truncheon, and returned to the cottage. He roused 60 year old Mrs Ellis, telling her that her husband had been wounded by poachers. Waller led Mrs Ellis along a lane leading in a direction away from the spot where he had left the body of her husband and shot her, finally beating her to death with the broken truncheon. Waller was charged with the wilful murder of Mr and Mrs Ellis. When he was first imprisoned, Joseph had scratched a picture of Keepers Cottage on the wall of his cell and wrote underneath 'Joseph Waller, murderer'.

Waller had been a police officer himself but had been dismissed for disorderly conduct. What transpired from Mrs Waller's testimony was that her son had suffered a blow to his head, while performing his duties as a policeman and had lain unconscious in St Bartholomew's hospital for three weeks some years earlier. For the last three years he had been in St Luke's Asylum having threatened her violently. Waller was declared insane at the Maidstone assizes and returned to St Luke's.

The funeral of the victims took place at St Nicholas church. Earl Sydney attended as a mourner accompanied by Mr Berens and local magistrates. Mr Lord, the stationmaster, and many others formed a long procession from Keepers Cottage to the churchyard. Canon Murray conducted the service and the two bodies were buried in one grave. (The grave is very well distinguished with a gabled top approximately four rows west of the mortuary shed).

The clergymen and police remained at the graveside for nearly an hour, arranging for people to pass by and pay their respects. Before and after the funeral a great many people

Above: Keeper's Cottage in Pettswood.

visited the cottage and woods and took cuttings from the trees and hedges. Photographs of the place were selling freely and there was an eager demand for memorial cards which had been printed for the occasion. The news of this very sad story was reported far and wide and even found its way into the Australian press.

5. Crowns and Coronets

DID YOU KNOW THAT...?

1. Queen Victoria visited Chislehurst on four separate occasions.
2. The last emperor of France died in Chislehurst and the building of his lasting memorial created neighbourly entrenchment, which was later regretted.
3. 40,000 mourners attended the funeral of the Prince Imperial of France here in 1879.

It is known that Queen Elizabeth I came to Chislehurst in July 1597 and stayed overnight at Scadbury; however Chislehurst has had many royal visits over the years, not least the 1870s when the exiled French Emperor Louis Napoleon III and his family lived here. Queen Victoria first visited Chislehurst on 30 November 1870 to greet the exiled French Empress, Eugenie, at Camden Place.

The Prince of Wales, later King Edward VII, called at Camden Place in March 1871 soon after the Emperor's arrival. He was to return for more sombre occasions: the funerals of the Emperor in 1873, The Prince Imperial in 1879 and that of Earl Sydney in 1890.

Queen Victoria was, in fact, not an infrequent visitor to Chislehurst. She made her second visit on 3 April 1871 and a third on 20 April 1872 where she was greeted by enthusiastic crowds on her way to Scadbury escorted by Earl Sydney, her Lord Chamberlain. Local rumour has it that there is a foot tunnel at Chislehurst Station rather than a bridge in order to protect the privacy of the ladies heading for the London bound platforms. It is far more likely that special arrangements were made for royal visitors and carriages would have been diverted to the accessible downside platforms anyway. The Queen's final visit was in 1879 when she stayed with the Empress at Camden Place during the funeral of the Prince Imperial.

Other royal visitors have followed. The Duchess of Albany, Queen Victoria's daughter-in-law, came to Chislehurst in June 1898 and 1913 to raise funds for the Albany Institute in Deptford and opened Albany Road as part of her splendid tour. Queen Mary, the wife of George V, visited Farringtons School on more than one occasion and also came to visit the Governesses Institute, as did her daughter-in-law, Queen Elizabeth the Queen Mother when it became Queen Mary House. Pictures of the future Princess Diana visiting Chislehurst have also emerged from the archives of Queen Mary's House.

The Death of the Last Emperor of France

Louis Napoleon Bonaparte, nephew of Napoleon Bonaparte, became President of France in 1849 and declared himself Emperor Napoleon III in 1853. He was deposed in 1870 after the Battle of Sedan in the Franco-Prussian war.

His wife, the Empress Eugenie and their son, the Prince Imperial, escaped to England, where they were offered Camden Place as a home by Nathaniel Strode, to the Empress's apparent surprise. Strode, a solicitor, had owned Camden Place since 1860 and had spent large sums of money transforming it into a French style chateau. He also managed a trust fund settled on the son of Elizabeth Howard, who had had a liaison with Louis Napoleon during an earlier visit to England. It later transpired that Strode received 900,000 francs from the Emperor during this time. In the 1830s, Louis Napoleon formed an attachment with a young English beauty, Emily Rowles, whose father owned Camden Place at the time. Louis Napoleon had often visited her there. It is, therefore, not so surprising that the Imperial family came to Chislehurst.

On 20 March 1871 the exiled Emperor, who had been imprisoned in Wilhelmshohe after his defeat at Sedan, joined his wife at Camden Place, arriving at Chislehurst by train. For two years, the French court made the village the fashionable place to be, but the Emperor died at Camden Place on 9 January 1873. He was only sixty-four.

On 15 December 1872, the Emperor had consulted Sir William Gull, Sir James Paget and Sir Henry Thompson concerning long-standing symptoms of stones in his bladder. On 2 January, Sir Henry performed an operation to destroy the stones. There was a further lithotripsy (physical destruction of hardened mass via the urethra) on 6 January but the Emperor died on the 9th at 10.45 a.m. This multistage operation was extremely painful and chloroform was used. There have been rumours that too much caused his demise but as can be seen from the death certificate, a copy of which hangs in the entrance hall of Camden Place to this day, the cause of death is stated as Calculus (kidney stones); renal disease; lithotrity seven days and exhaustion.

On the Sunday after his death, some privileged visitors were admitted to the bedroom to view the Emperor's body. The room was very dark, the coffin stood on trestles in the middle of the floor, and the body, clothed in the uniform last worn at Sedan, lay unshrouded in the coffin. Some who viewed the dead man remarked on the wearied aspects of his features, others said that death had removed many of the lines of anxiety and sorrow.

The funeral service took place at St Mary's Roman Catholic Church on 15 January where thousands of visitors assembled. A deputation of workmen, with the French tricolour, led the way; then seven priests, bareheaded and chanting as they walked followed by the hearse with its nodding horses' plumes. The Prince Imperial, as chief mourner, walked alone, immediately behind. He was followed by the Princes Lucien and Joseph Bonaparte; Princes Murat, and the younger scions of the house of Bonaparte; and then senators; nobles; ambassadors; deputies; and others, amounting to some 2,000 people. Of these, only a privileged few were allowed to enter the church. The funeral service lasted an hour and twenty minutes. Children chanted the 'Agnus Dei' and the rolling strains of the 'Miserere'.

Death of the Prince Imperial

The Anglo-Zulu War in South Africa of 1879 had the aim of creating a federation of African kingdoms in an attempt to extend British influence over a repressed black majority. The war's most well-known battle was the successful defence of Rorke's Drift by 100 British and Colonial troops against 3, to 4,000 Zulu warriors, at the price of the lives of 600 Zulus before the Zulus were decisively defeated at the Battle of Ulundi on 4 July. It was a hollow victory as fighting and bloodshed continued in the ensuing years.

One significant casualty of the war was the twenty-three-year-old Prince Imperial, Napoleon Eugene Louis Jean Joseph Bonaparte, only son of the widowed Empress Eugenie of France.

The Prince had been educated at the Royal Military Academy at Woolwich and had begged his mother to be able to see some military action. He was eventually allowed to go to Africa, but only in the role of an observer. On 1 June 1879 the prince was attached to the cavalry corps on the northern frontier of Zululand and while out on a surveying expedition the prince's party was subject to a surprise attack by the Zulus. The prince, who had slipped accidentally from his horse, was attacked while attempting to escape on foot and he was killed. When his body was found, naked in a gulley, there were eighteen assegai (spear) wounds to his body and only the religious icons around his neck remained.

Right: The Prince Imperial Monument at Chislehurst Common.

Lord Sydney was sent, by special request of Queen Victoria, to break the news to the Empress at Camden Place. In the village all the tradesmen showed their respect by closing their shutters. The prince's body was embalmed and brought back to England for burial with his father at St Mary's, Chislehurst.

On the day of the funeral Chislehurst witnessed, for a second time, a funeral on an even grander scale than that of the Emperor six years earlier, with an estimated crowd of 40,000. On 12 July 1879 the gun carriage was escorted by the Royal Regiment of Artillery from Woolwich. The Queen, with her son Prince Leopold and daughter Princess Beatrice, visited the Empress by special train to Chislehurst. The Prince of Wales and his brothers were pall bearers.

A committee, whose secretary and treasurer was Mr T. R. Watts of The Briars, after whom Watts Lane is named, set up an appeal which resulted in the building of the granite Celtic cross, designed by Edward Robson, on the common by the 'Dwellers of Chislehurst' in 1880. At the time there was some local opposition to what was seen as an encroachment on the common, which were not then statutorily protected and at what was seen as a Catholic project in a Protestant parish. The road across the common formerly known as Station Road was subsequently renamed Prince Imperial Road.

The cross bears the words of the prince himself extracted from his will, 'That I should die with a sentiment of profound gratitude for her Majesty the Queen of England, for all the Royal Family and for the Country where I have received during eight years such cordial hospitality.'

The cross is now a scheduled monument and is cared for by the Trustees of Chislehurst Commons. The monument displays the Bonaparte emblems of bees and violets.

French emblems on the Prince Imperial monument.

The bee symbolised immortality and resurrection and was used to link the new dynasty to the origins of France. Golden bees were discovered in the tomb of Childeric in 457 and considered to be the oldest emblem of France. Eagles were the other prominent emblem of Imperial France and can still be seen on St Mary's chapel.

The Empress left Chislehurst for Farnborough, Hampshire in early 1881. She returned only once to attend the funeral of Lord Sydney in 1890. She is known to have visited the place in Africa where the Prince was killed, on 25 May 1880, where a cross had been placed to mark the spot where the Prince fell. She planted a willow and ivy from Camden Place in the ground.

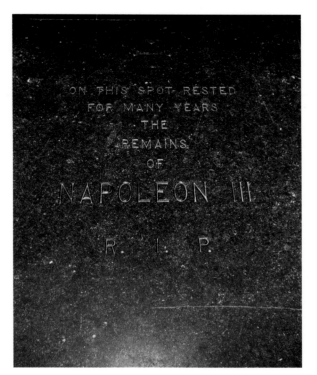

Right: The memorial slab in St Mary's church dedicated to Emperor Napoleon III.

Potential Mausoleum

Having witnessed two funerals on a grand scale it may come as a surprise to discover that there are no deceased Imperial royals in Chislehurst today.

Initially, a small chapel was built on the side of St Mary's church, designed by local architect and Catholic convert, Henry Clutton, who took no fee for his work. The chapel was completed by the end of 1873 and Eugenie arranged for Louis Napoleon's tomb to be transferred from the main nave into the chapel. The tomb, a Scottish granite sarcophagus was a gift from Queen Victoria. Officially the chapel was open to the public but for the first five years it was principally a private space for the Empress and Prince Imperial to mourn their loss; a small exterior door on the west wall offered them direct access to the chapel.

Above: Stone eagle on the roof of St Mary's church.

When the Prince Imperial was killed in Zululand in 1879, Eugenie instructed French architect, Destailleur, to design a mausoleum and as the months passed the vision grew all the more elaborate, planning to turn the whole church into a monastery. Eugenie's plans worried the resident priest, Monsignor Goddard. He anticipated that these exalted ideas would arouse the potential anger of the church's neighbours and landowners: the Edlmann family, who were Protestant. Monsignor Goddard was increasingly upset by what he deemed 'a peep show', his church being visited by 'Sunday crowds of reactionists', people were quite used to coming in during a service, walking to the tomb, staring and marching out again.

Eugenie found a solution by purchasing 257 acres at Farnborough in Hampshire where the mausoleum, St Michael's Abbey, was built. The bodies of the Emperor and his son were removed from St Mary's church on 9 January 1888, taken with full military honours to Chislehurst Station to be conveyed by special train to Farnborough.

Chislehurst's Imperial interlude was over and the only person buried beneath the memorial chapel is Captain Henry Bowden, the Catholic convert, who commissioned the building of the church in the first place. The chapel was built over the land where he lies.

The final twist in the story comes in the form of a codicil in the will of Frederick Joseph Edlmann in 1890, where he expressed regret at not having sold some of his land to the Empress.

Napoleonic architectural features at St Mary's church.

As a more cheerful aside, one can visit St Mary's and admire the Napoleonic symbolism and those who use the inner sanctum of the presbytery can appreciate the 'throne room' with leftover tiles on the floor!

6. Characters

There are many residents of renown who were born, lived and/or died in Chislehurst. Many are well known and their stories often told: William Willett, who instigated British Summer Time, Sir John Lubbock who introduced Bank Holidays, and Sir Malcolm Campbell who raced to better his times on both land and water. However, there are others who left their mark and are not as well known.

Dr Charles West, 1816–1898

Founder of Great Ormond Street Hospital for Sick Children

The words on his Chislehurst grave in St Mary's churchyard read: 'A man of great mental gifts and a truly noble heart who devoted his life with rare unselfishness to the alleviation of human suffering and who has left a permanent memorial of faithful and fruitful work in the first children's hospital in England.'

A second plaque on the grave was given by The Hospital of Sick Children, Great Ormond Street, London and reads: 'Remembered by all whose lives have been changed by his inspiring vision. Founded by him in 1852. The best a man can offer, To the Love of God be Sure, Is Kindness to his Little Ones, And Bounty to the Poor'.

Charles West was born in London in August 1816 and began his medical career at Amersham in 1831 entering St Bartholomew's as a medical student in 1833 where he won prizes in his exams. He went on to Bonn University finally qualifying as a doctor in Paris in 1837. He returned to London and worked at St Bartholomew's as well as the Infirmary for Children in Waterloo Road. He worked at the Middlesex Hospital from 1845, specialising in midwifery training before focusing on this work at St Bartholomew's for the next twelve years. He tried to convert a dispensary at Waterloo Road into a children's specialist hospital but there was opposition from his fellow doctors. Finally, after several disappointments, he opened Great Ormond Street Hospital in February 1852 where, for the next twenty-three years, he was the chief physician.

Dr West converted to Catholicism in 1877 and experienced some difficulties with the chairman of the board at Great Ormond Street which caused him to leave the hospital. He left London altogether in 1880 to live abroad; he was an asthmatic and suffered when the weather was foggy and damp. He practiced in Nice during the winters. It was on his return from there in 1898 that he collapsed in Paris and died.

At his own specific request, he was buried in St Mary's churchyard. It is not known why he would have wanted this. His children did not live locally and his second wife was French with no obvious Chislehurst connection. The fame of the little church however with its French Imperial connections was well known. Reverend Boone, the incumbent at the time, had worked in the poorer London parishes and had connections in France. It was he that conducted West's funeral so it is possible that there had been a personal connection between the two men.

Left: Grave of Dr Charles West, founder of Great Ormond Street Hospital.

Canon Francis Murray, 1820–1902

Compiler of Hymns Ancient and Modern

Francis Murray was born on the Isle of Man in 1820 and became rector at St Nicholas church in 1846 and remained in Chislehurst until his death in 1902. He lived at The

Rectory, opposite the church where The Glebe now stands. He is most famous for a little book which sold 30 million copies, *Hymns Ancient and Modern* compiled largely by him and conceived in a railway carriage of the Great Western Railway.

In the summer of 1858 Murray was travelling with Revd William Denton, editor of *The Church Hymnal*. They were discussing hymn books and resolved during the course of the journey to produce a collection of the very best music that was then available.

An advertisement placed in the *Guardian* newspaper in October 1858 attracted a widespread response. Material poured in to be passed around for comment, criticism, and altered to fit an 'excellent tune'. Thirteen proprietors, Murray was one of them, put up the money for publication in 1861. He did not write any of the hymns, his role seems to have been more about writing 'apologetic and placatory letters' to the contributors, of which there had to be many.

By 1894, *Ancient and Modern* was being used in 70 per cent of churches in the country as well as schools, the armed services and in private homes. The first edition sold 4.5 million copies in the first eight years and when a second edition was published with the addition of music, a million copies were sold on day one. In Chislehurst, Canon Murray used his share of the proceeds to endow the Church of the Annunciation in the heart of the village. There is no doubt that by the time of Murray's death in 1902, *Hymns Ancient and Modern* was almost a national institution. He is buried in St Nicholas churchyard and there is a plaque inside the church to commemorate the publication.

Frederick Richard Simms, 1863–1944

Frederick Simms was an engineer, inventor, and, as a pioneer for motor cars, he became a leading figure in the early British motor industry. Simms and his second wife lived in Chislehurst from 1915 until his death in 1944, at a house called Storth Oaks next to Waratah in Walden Road. The house is no longer there.

Simms was born in Germany and, as a young man, he completed an engineering apprenticeship. He became a friend of Gottlieb Daimler and in 1893 he purchased the rights to manufacture petrol engines for boats from Daimler and formed the Daimler Motor Syndicate Ltd. This is believed to be the UK's first petrol motor company. In 1900 Simms established his own vehicle manufacturing company, Simms Manufacturing Co. at Kilburn, where a wide range of vehicles was produced.

As well as his engineering skills, Simms was a leading advocate for the newly invented motor cars. The car industry that developed in Britain can be said to have begun through his efforts. In 1895, with his friend the Hon. Evelyn Ellis, Simms took the first petrol driven horseless carriage ride on English roads – illegal at the time. He took part in the Emancipation Run between London and Brighton in 1896 which was to celebrate the emancipation of horseless vehicles from the severe restrictions previously placed on their use. This is now the annual London to Brighton Run.

Simms founded the Motor Car Club in 1896; the Automobile Club in 1897 (which became the Royal Automobile Club (RAC) 10 years later); and the Society of Motor Manufacturers and Traders in 1902.

Simm's ashes are placed at a memorial just inside the Lychgate of the Annunciation Church.

C. B. Fry, 1872–1956

Possibly the greatest all-rounder of them all. A very remarkable human being

Charles Burgess Fry was briefly a resident of Chislehurst. Chiefly known for his sporting prowess he is the only man to have captained England in both cricket and football. He held the long jump record for twenty-one years and played rugby for The Barbarians. He became a politician; diplomat; academic; teacher; writer; editor and publisher, and he was even interviewed for the vacant throne of Albania in 1921.

Born in Croydon in 1872, his family moved to Southill Road, Chislehurst when he was very young. He wrote in his memoirs that he could remember the sound of the trains rumbling along the embankment at Elmstead Woods. From a map of the ownership of the plots of land in the road, the house was probably Camden Wood Cottage, later St Andrews, but it is now demolished. He remembered at a tender age walking in the Camden Estate Park with his nanny and having brief conversations with the widowed Empress Eugenie and the Prince Imperial. He recalled his shock at learning of the young prince's death in the Zulu Wars 'someone I knew very well has died' he said.

The family moved to Orpington when he was seven but he was a weekly boarder at Hornbrook House School. He recalled the start of one cricket practice, in about 1880, when an obstinate Scot refused to be given out. The player grabbed the stump and ball and ran in the direction of Bromley. Fry and his friends gave chase and they all ended up returning to Chislehurst in the postman's van.

He died in Hampstead on 7 September 1956.

Richmal Crompton, 1891–1969

Author of the Just William *books*

Richmal Crompton Lamburn was born in Bury, Lancashire, on 15 November 1890. As an adult after four years teaching in Lancashire, she moved to Bromley in 1917, where she taught classics for five years at Bromley High School.

Her teaching career finished at the end of 1923 when she contracted polio, which caused her to lose the use of her right leg. She was already writing short stories while teaching. Initially published in *Happy Mag*, a number of short stories were published in a book, called *Just William*. In addition to her *William* books, she published four other children's books, and fifty novels, or collections of short stories, intended for adults, although none of these had the success of her *William* books.

After the huge success of the *William* books, Richmal was able to purchase an acre of land in Oakley Road, Bromley, where she had a house built, The Glebe, which now sports a blue heritage plaque in her honour.

In the early 1950s, she looked for a smaller house, and in 1954 she moved to live at Beechworth, a house in Chislehurst on Orpington Road, at the top of Leesons Hill. She continued her writing here, and became involved in the local community, as a church goer and supporter of the Conservative Party. She also became interested in reincarnation, mysticism and the occult.

Above: Richmal Crompton with her great-nephew, Edward Ashbee.

By the time she came to live in Chislehurst she had published twenty-eight *William* books. The last of her thirty-nine *William* books was published in 1970, the year after her death. Given that she never married and taught at a girls school, what was the inspiration for the misdemeanours for William and the gang? She had a brother but it was her nephew, Tommy Disher, a pupil at St Hugh's Bickley, who was considered to be her inspiration. Her great-nephew Edward Ashbee was a further influence.

She died in Farnborough Hospital on 11 January 1969 aged seventy-eight. Her funeral was held at St Nicholas church, followed by cremation at Eltham.

Alan Wilson Watts, 1915–1973

Perhaps the foremost western interpreter of eastern thought for the modern world.

New York Times

Alan Watts was born on 6 January 1915 at No. 3 (now No. 5), Holbrook Lane, Chislehurst. The only child of Laurence and Emily Watts. His mother, a devout Christian whose father had been a missionary, was a designer and teacher at the Royal School of Needlework. His father, worked for the Michelin Tyre Co.

Their home was described by Watts in his autobiography as 'a pretty little cottage in a rather attractive suburb of London, with acres of unspoiled common land, a village of

Right: Alan Watts.

old-world shops, a fine old church, St Nicholas, and a village pond'. The cottage was tiny, with a front door that opened on to a flight of stairs, a dining room and kitchen on the right of the door, a sitting room on the left. Upstairs were two bedrooms and a small bathroom with lavatory and hot water geyser. They planted a rowan tree in the front garden and called the house Rowan Tree Cottage. Alan's memoirs recall a garden full of tomatoes, raspberries and beans on sticks, stretching far above his head. He also has a vivid memory of an enormous sycamore tree, ninety feet high on the boundary between Farringtons and their garden.

He attended St Nicholas kindergarten, next door to the church, taught by Miss Nicholas. Aged seven, he was enrolled as a weekly boarder at St Hugh's prep school in Bickley, he travelled by bus each week with his mother.

As Alan grew up and travelled, he commented that Chislehurst Station, with its knock-knock sound of tickets being issued and a tring of the bell announcing an approaching train, was 'a centre of liberation!'

In 1928 Alan won a scholarship to King's School, Canterbury where he joined the debating society and spoke for the first time on Zen Buddhism and its rituals. Alan failed his Oxford University scholarship exam, deliberately it seems, and at seventeen went to work in a printing house and then a bank.

Above: Rowan Tree Cottage, Holbrook Lane.

He began to move in theosophical circles and was absorbed by meetings in Soho restaurants, on one occasion missing the 11.55 a.m. last train from Charing Cross, and ending up being sent home in a chauffeur driven limousine belonging to Dmitrije Mitrinovic, a self-styled guru from Yugoslavia.

Watts published his first book *The Spirit of Zen* when he was nineteen. There was to be second edition twenty years later. He read and wrote Mandarin, practiced martial arts and trained himself in calligraphy. In 1937 he published *The Legacy of Asia and Western Man*, described by the *Church Times* as a 'witty little book'.

He was by this time leading a bohemian lifestyle, and met Eleanor, the daughter of Ruth Fuller Everett, an American Buddhist. They had an engagement party at Rowan Tree Cottage the day before they sailed to New York in 1937. When they married back in England in April 1938, Eleanor was already pregnant. They returned to New York just before the war. In America Watts lectured at the Jungian Club and wrote *The Meaning of Happiness*. He wrote articles and renewed his interest in Christianity. He was ordained as an Anglican Priest, and ministered in Chicago. During this time he wrote *Behold the Spirit* and was awarded a master's degree. His services were popular if elaborate, but his ministry ended in scandal, following revelations about marital problems and a *ménage a quatre*!

He returned then to his earlier passion for Zen. His next book was *The Wisdom of Insecurity*. He moved his daughters to San Francisco and taught at the Academy of Asia Studies. But Watts was a neglectful father and when his parents visited in 1952 they returned to Chislehurst with their younger granddaughter, Anne aged 10, who attended Farringtons for the next eight years.

In 1957 Watts wrote his most famous book *The Way of Zen*. He went on to write *Nature – Man and Woman*. In 1958, en route to lecture in Zurich, Watts returned briefly to Chislehurst finding it unchanged, there were still the same adverts painted on metal sheets at the station – Stephen's ink and Palethorpe's sausages – the old high street contained the same sweet shop, the chemist still run by the same owners, and Alan would still walk past the church to *The Tiger's Head* for a drink with his father.

In the 1960s the emergence of the counter-culture coincided with a radical change in Watts' own life. He left his second wife, Dorothy, then pregnant with her fifth child, and went to live with his new love, Jano, on an old ferry boat in Marin County. His 1962 book *The Joyous Cosmology* was a treatise on LSD as a kind of medicine for sick modern men. By 1967, the Summer of Love, he was a counter-culture celebrity lecturing in the US and Europe and one of the most revered public figures in a worldwide revolution. He drank heavily and his sexual adventures took their toll on his third marriage.

He did not return to Chislehurst when his mother died in 1961 but came back in 1968 to help his father move to a retirement home, Merevale. His last visit to Chislehurst was in 1970 for his father's ninetieth birthday party at The Tiger's Head, and Watts sang the Pete Seeger song, 'Little Boxes'.

Watts died of heart failure in California, in 1973, aged only fifty-eight; his body was cremated in a Buddhist ceremony shortly afterwards. His legacy continues to this day at the Alan Watts Mountain Center, north of San Francisco, his works remain widely broadcast and discussed.

Sir Victor George Shepheard, KCB, RCNC, 1983–1989

Designer of the HMY Britannia

Victor George Shepheard was born on 21 March 1893 and, from an apprenticeship at HM Dockyard Devonport, he became a cadet to the Royal Naval College, Greenwich graduating in 1915 and joined the Grand Fleet as an engineer lieutenant.

He was present at the Battle of Jutland 1916 in the dreadnought *Agincourt* as a damage control officer, an experience which stayed with him for the rest of his life. 'It was a magnificent sight,' he later recalled. 'That terrific fleet of 150 ships all steaming together, we shall never see anything like it again.'

Shepheard was professor of naval architecture at Greenwich from 1934 to 1939. At the outbreak of the Second World War he joined the naval construction department, in Bath, as chief constructor, rising to assistant director in 1942 and deputy director in 1947. In 1952 he became the director of naval construction. The quiet Porpoise-class submarine, the guided missile ships of the County-class, the first gas-turbine ships of the Tribal-class and, eventually, the Dreadnought nuclear submarine programme all benefited from his design skills. However, the ship of which he was most proud was the Royal Yacht *Britannia*, designed in 1952. Sir Victor was a frequent visitor to Buckingham Palace as the King and other members of the Royal Family took a keen interest in the design.

Shepheard was made Companion of The Most Honourable Order of the Bath in 1950 and created KCB in 1954. He was also a Chevalier of the Legion d'Honneur, an acknowledgement by the French government of his wartime work on the Mulberry Harbour, part of the Normandy Landings.

He lived in Manor Park, Chislehurst, from 1959 until his death at the age of ninety-six in 1989.

Ted Willis, 1918–1992

Holbrook Lane runs off Shepherds Green, a small green, part of the common on which stands a group of Arts and Crafts houses; No. 5 sports a heritage plaque commemorating the life of Lord Ted Willis.

Edward Henry Willis was born in Tottenham. He was politically active in the Labour Party and became General Secretary of the Young Communist League in 1941. He married Audrey Hale in 1944 and had a son and a daughter. In 1949, in collaboration with an Australian, Willis sent an unpublished play about the London Police to Ealing Studios. It was called *The Blue Lamp*. The spin off series *Dixon of Dock Green* ran for twenty-two years from 1953 and became a British institution. Another successful TV series that he wrote was *The Adventures of Black Beauty*. He had a charismatic personality and was an excellent public speaker.

The family moved to Holbrook Lane in 1959. Willis was created a life peer by Harold Wilson in 1963 taking the title Baron Chislehurst. He died at home of a coronary on 22 September 1992.

Heritage plaques honouring Sir Victor
Shepheard (*above*) and Lord Ted Willis
(*right*).

7. Conflict

DID YOU KNOW THAT...?

1. Chislehurst's big houses were rapidly converted into Red Cross hospitals run by local women from 1914 to 1918.
2. Chislehurst Caves were used to store tons of high explosives during the Great War.
3. Children rescued from Prague in 1938 were housed in Chislehurst, a local kindertransport mission that is recalled by a local plaque on a bench to this day.

The Great War, 1914–18

Where lives changed for women too

Chislehurst made an invaluable contribution to the war effort. Ten grand houses were hastily converted into hospitals by the Red Cross, to care for the wounded from the Western Front. At the centre of operations was Abbey Lodge in Lubbock Road. It is a remarkable survivor of a bygone age.

In 1912 a meeting had been called by a Dr Allan to set up a Voluntary Aid Detachment (VAD) for local residents to support the care of wounded soldiers. As a result the Red Cross Unit Kent 60 was set up, staffed by VADs initially under the leadership of Miss Margaret Alston from Rosemount on Cricket Ground Road and, subsequently, by Miss Beatrix Batten from Lower Camden.

War was declared on 4 August 1914 and orders to mobilise the hospitals came at midnight on 13 October. Lubbock Road began its new role with the return of the wounded from the Front. Christ Church Hall had twenty-five beds ready by 6.00 a.m. on the 14th, thirty-three wounded Belgian soldiers arrived at 9.00 a.m. The less seriously wounded were sent to co-ed Bel, a girl's school further down the road. The headmistress, Miss Fox, allowed the use of the sanatorium with eight beds. That sanatorium still exists today, as Willow Lodge. Two days later, instructions were received to prepare for more patients, Abbey Lodge was mobilised with the arrival of thirty more wounded coming by train.

Reverend Pole, the vicar of Christ Church had given his parish room at 'great inconvenience' but four of his daughters rose to the nursing challenge. Muriel, twenty; Hilda, twenty-one; and Gladys, eighteen. His eldest daughter, thirty-one-year-old Lily, became quartermaster.

Each VAD volunteer was given a note which read:

Above: Abbey Lodge.

Below: Awaiting the arrival of the wounded. Chislehurst Station, October 1914.

You have to perform tasks which will need your courage, your energy, your patience, your humility, your determination to overcome all difficulties. It will be your duty not only to set an example of discipline and perfect steadiness of character, but also to maintain the most courteous relations with those whom you are helping in this great struggle. Sacrifices may be asked of you. Give generously and wholeheartedly, grudging nothing, but remembering that you are giving because your country needs your help.

Christ Church 'hospital' moved to Brooklyn, a house further down the road, where Ross Court stands now.

Lammas, further up the road, became a VAD hospital, being an auxiliary unit of the Ontario Hospital at Orpington, remaining in use until 1919. Hillside, next door, was also utilised from September 1918 to March 1919.

Oak House in Holbrook Lane (opposite) was a VAD hospital from 1914 until 1916 and was run by the newly formed Kent 66. It was lent to the British Red Cross as a convalescent hospital by the owner Mr Cyril Heywood. It had thirty-five beds and opened on 14 October 1914 with the first wounded Belgian soldiers arriving on that day just a few hours after preparations for the hospital were completed.

Heywood, a director of the family varnish business, had married Phyllis, the daughter of local magistrate Robert Leonard Powell in 1912. Their married home was the newly-built Oak House, No. 45 Holbrook Lane, designed by local architect E. J. May. Sadly Phyllis died in childbirth in 1913. Cyril remarried in 1916, the second Mrs Heywood requiring the return of their property. As a result the hospital closed in July 1916 and the patients transferred to the Gorse Auxiliary Hospital in Manor Road. Oak House has since changed its name to Antokil, and is today a care home for Polish residents.

On 16 October 1914 instructions were given to prepare another fifty-bed auxiliary hospital with an operating theatre at Hornbrook House on the High Street, which had been a boy's prep school. The hospital closed in August 1918 and became a YMCA. The building was demolished in 1970 and is now a car park.

Hollington House, next door, owned by Mr and Mrs Teichman became another hospital with forty beds. The original house was demolished and replaced by Hollington Court. Local people offered time; garden parties; music and entertainment; use of their cars; and refreshments for the new arrivals. This was often in the middle of the night and local newspaper reports praise the self-sacrifice and devotion of Chislehurst's residents.

Over 10,000 injured soldiers were cared for in Chislehurst under the command of Miss Beatrix Batten. She was to give a lifetime's service to the Red Cross becoming, in later years, County Director for Kent and received the CBE. There is a memorial bench to her memory on the Common near Heathfield Lane, looking towards Prickend Pond (shown opposite).

Ethel Bilbrough's First World War Diary

Ethel Mary Dixon, born 1868, married, Kenneth Bilbrough in 1897, a marine insurance executive. They moved to Elmstead Grange in 1904; it was a grand house surrounded by 22 acres of land (shown overleaf). It is now Babington House School, Grange Road.

At the outbreak of the First World War Ethel, by then in her mid-forties and a keen writer to national newspapers, was also a diarist. She recorded her thoughts about what it was like to live through this transformative war. It is full of Ethel's own idiosyncratic opinions. She wrote,

Above: The home of Ethel Bilbrough.

It seems to me that everyone who happens to be alive in such epoch stirring times ought to write something of what is going on! Just think how interesting it would be to read in years' hence when peace once more reigns supreme, and everything has settled down to its usual torpid routine of dullness.

In May 1915 she wrote,

The latest excitement has been the Daylight Saving Bill. Some years ago the originator of the scheme, one Willett by name, who lived at Chislehurst, tried hard to get the Government to adopt it, but with their usual dislike of venturing on anything new (even should it be of the utmost benefit to mankind) they would have none of it. But now poor Willett has been in his grave some months, and as the war has brought home to our stupid Government the utmost need of saving coal and gas, the bill was not only thought advisable, but brought in and passed. So on Saturday night, or rather on Sunday morning, 21 May, at 2 o'clock, all clocks and watches had to be set on 3 o'clock! We altered all our time pieces however at 9.30 p.m. on Saturday evening, and then went to bed as we had made it 10.30 p.m.! So we got all night without difficulty and without any loss of sleep though there were several in England who raised objections. We benefit in many ways by the new arrangement ... it is broad daylight until close on ten and instead of having to get the gas lit and sit indoors reading, one can go for a good walk, or do some gardening, or indulge in other daylight occupation. Taking it all round, everyone has reason to bless the name Willett!

The Bilbroughs retired to Wiltshire where Ethel passed away aged eighty-four. Kenneth lived for a further twenty-two years.

Ethel's diary was found in a clear-out by Kenneth's second wife, Elsie, who gifted it to the Imperial War Museum. We will either have to forgive or commend her for writing that 'Chislehurst is an extremely correct and proper suburb'. This was, in fact, in reference to the way in which wounded soldiers behaved themselves when venturing out into the village, or rather into the pubs.

Victoria Cross Recipient George Allen Maling, 1888–1929

The Victoria Cross (VC) is awarded for 'most conspicuous bravery, or some daring or pre-eminent act of valour or self-sacrifice or extreme devotion to duty in the presence of the enemy'. 628 awards of the VC were made during The Great War, 454 of them to British-born recipients.

In Chislehurst Cemetery at the end of Beaverwood Road lies one recipient. Captain George Allen Maling. The youngest son of a doctor, he was born 6 October 1888 in Bishopwearmouth, County Durham. He was educated at Uppingham (at the same time as another renowned resident of Chislehurst, Sir Malcolm Campbell). He studied medicine at Exeter College, Oxford and St Thomas's Hospital and graduated in 1914. He was commissioned with the Royal Army Medical Corps attached to the 12th Battalion Rifle Brigade.

Chislehurst Cemetery chapel, Beareswood Road.

As mentioned in dispatches on 25 September 1915 near Fauquissart in France, following the Battle of Loos, a group of British soldiers were trapped in a ruin in no-man's land. Under an artillery barrage, Maling shouldered his medical pack, shouted for his orderly and jumped the parapet, running through a curtain of exploding steel and arrived at the ruin unharmed.

Maling moved from casualty to casualty, dressing wounds, carrying the less seriously wounded to more comfortable positions and giving palliative care to the fatally wounded. He worked for over twenty-four hours with untiring energy, collecting and treating in the open, over 300 casualties under repeated heavy shell fire. He was temporarily stunned by the bursting of a large high explosive shell which wounded his orderly and killed several soldiers. A second shell covered him and his instruments with debris, but he continued his work single handed. By 8.00 a.m. on the following day, the German gunners ceased their bombardment and British rescue teams were able to bring the wounded back to the casualty stations.

The VC was presented to Captain Maling on 15 January 1916 by King George V at Buckingham Palace. He served for a short time at the military hospital in Grantham. He married Daisy Wolmer, from Winnipeg, Canada in 1917 and returned to France for two years with the 34th Field Ambulance of the 11th Division. When asked to comment on the action that won him the medal he modestly said he had nothing to add.

At the end of the war he worked at the Victoria Hospital for Children in Chelsea before being appointed as a surgeon to outpatients at St John's Hospital, Lewisham.

He died on 9 July 1929 aged forty, in Lee, South East London. Chislehurst was most probably the nearest available burial place in wartime London.

Grave of Captain George Allen Maling VC.

Chislehurst Caves

In the early 1900s the caves were owned by Ernest Wythes, the grandson of railway magnate George Wythes, who had lived at Bickley Hall and built the water tower at the entrance of his estate on the top of Summer Hill. At this time Ernest had moved to Copped Hall, Essex.

Formerly chalk mines, the caves were a tourist attraction; visitors took tea on the lawns of The Bickley Hotel and then entered the underground passages to see for themselves the tunnels and workings.

During the First World War the twenty-two-mile-long series of tunnels carved underground was pressed into service to store ammunition from Woolwich Arsenal. Special trains conveyed 25,000 lb of explosives to and from the Arsenal and unloaded at Chislehurst Station via the goods yard. Lorries were then used to transport the explosives to the caves and a narrow gauge railway was laid to access the deepest parts of the caves. 500 metres of railway track were laid with four cast iron turntables to manoeuvre the munitions trucks efficiently. The men themselves were exposed to many hazards, and suffered burns and jaundice caused by the chemicals in the munitions.

Special sections of these tunnels highlight a unique series of carvings that munitions workers made in the soft chalk to honour the memory of Nurse Edith Cavell, who was captured and shot by the Germans in 1915. This particular incident was documented by Ethel Bilbrough in her diary.

Carving of Edith Cavell in the Chislehurst Caves.

Letters in the National Archives at Kew reveal that, at this time, there was an entrance to the caves in Dr Lawson's garden at Camden Rise, Old Hill which was guarded during the war. Another letter tells of a German family living at The Ivy House on Old Hill being 'removed'. It stated that 'no troops are billeted at this house and [...] danger from this source is not considered to be great', however the family were removed to 'an approved residence', no doubt interned by the authorities. We know from Arthur Battle's book that a German family lived in Lower Camden producing baked goods; recent photographic evidence has suggested their name was Zeigler.

A further letter reveals that two dogs accompanied the external cave patrols on their visits twice by day and twice by night. One dog in particular, was reported to be an 'excellent worker, investigating with great thoroughness, all the depressions where subsidence had occurred and weak spots where an unauthorised entry to the caves might be possible'.
After the war the narrow gauge railway was dismantled and sold.

Between the wars, the caves were brought by Kent Mushrooms Ltd, who still own them today. The high humidity and the constant temperature make the caves an ideal place to cultivate mushrooms. Modern production methods make the commercial growing of the crop untenable but mushrooms are still grown in small quantities.

The caves have long held fascination. W. J. Nicholls, who lived in Chislehurst, was Vice Principal of the British Archaeological Association and wrote the 1903 book *Chislehurst Caves and Dene Holes*, stating that 'these extensive underground galleries have been used in times of political and religious trouble and were one of the most remarkable sites to be found in this country'. However, this was refuted in 1924 by Arthur Bonner, a London printer who was a Fellow of the Society of Antiquaries, who undertook a survey and denounced Nicholls for having created 'caves of romance compared to caves of reality'.

Zeigler's delivery cart.

Mushrooms growing in Chislehurst Caves.

There is no archaeological evidence of druidic temples, granaries or sepulchres, slave prisons or places of early Christian dwellings of the ancient Britons as described by Nicholls. They are former chalk mines and the men who worked them were only anxious to get good chalk for lime burning and fertiliser.

It is a good story that, in April 1924, fourteen journalists were taken underground and, using Bonner's map, had to find their way out. A journalist from the *Daily Mail* was the last man out.

The least secret story of the caves is their time as the Chislehurst Hotel during the Blitz of the Second World War. The caves became Britain's largest public air raid shelter. Buses left Deptford at tea time returning the next morning; people from the East End of London arrived by train, and locals sheltered there overnight. People made the best of it, paying a penny for a pitch with only a curtain for privacy. The caves had electric lighting; toilets; a cinema; a chapel; a gym and even a dance floor. Between the autumn of 1940 and the spring of 1941 up to 8,000 people lived in the caves every night (see plaque opposite).

Second World War Kindertransport

There is a plaque on a bench at the corner of the junction of Lubbock Road with Old Hill. It is in gratitude to Rev and Mrs Davidson for their part in rescuing sixty-eight children from Central Europe in 1939 (see memorial bench opposite).

In 1938 Hitler marched into Czechoslovakia. The Barbican Mission for the Jews had a centre in Prague; Revd I. E. Davidson went there in early 1938. He was besieged by hundreds of families eager for an interview in the hope that their children who had claims to British nationality by having been born in England or had one British parent could gain the necessary authority to come to England.

It was agreed that fifty children could be taken to England but permits had to be arranged. There was at this time an organisation already in existence whose object it was to rescue children from Germany and later from Austria but Czechoslovakia had not been taken into consideration. There were weeks of delay but the fifty permits were eventually granted.

The problem of housing the children required considerable effort. Chislehurst was known to the mission as having many large houses which were dilapidated having been empty for years. Seven Trees in Lubbock Road was identified as suitable accommodation. The purchase was all but complete when a Lubbock Road resident objected.

His objection was published in the *Bromley Times*:

Friday 20 January 1939

Dear Sir,
Your readers in the locality will be interested in the following activity protesting against the invasion of foreigners.

The following letter was signed by thirty-one landlords and residents of Lubbock Road and forwarded to the Council: 'We the undersigned property owners and ratepayers strongly protest to the council against the proposed use of Seven Trees as a home for foreign refugees. It will greatly depreciate the sale value, amenities and rateable value

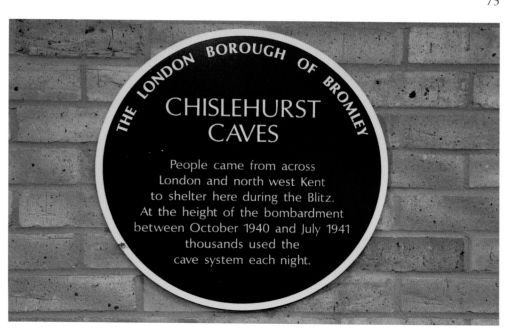

THE LONDON BOROUGH OF BROMLEY

CHISLEHURST CAVES

People came from across
London and north west Kent
to shelter here during the Blitz.
At the height of the bombardment
between October 1940 and July 1941
thousands used the
cave system each night.

Rev. & Mrs. I. E. DAVIDSON & FRIENDS
GRATEFULLY REMEMBERED BY
ALL THE BMJ CHILDREN
(68 OF THEM RESCUED FROM CENTRAL EUROPE 1939)

of all the properties in Lubbock Road and adjoining neighbourhood. Both house and garden are wholly unsuitable for such a purpose and quite inadequate for the fifty children and requisite attendants (as quoted in the press). Also its proximity to London in air raids should receive due consideration and we herewith record our protest against

any further proposal to utilise other premises in Lubbock Road for this purpose. We property owners and ratepayers claim the right of protection by the Council of our interests and consider that the residential district of Chislehurst is totally unsuitable for the purpose suggested.

However there were positive neighbours in the road too. Revd Davidson addressed a large meeting at Hatton House, further down the road. The Revd J. R. Carpenter of Christ Church was at the meeting and asked for money and household items to be sent direct to Revd Davidson. It was also helpful that the Chislehurst Refugee Association was actively homing children at another large house in the area, Seafield, on the common.

The Leader of the Council was a staunch ally and took up the matter on behalf of the mission. Revd Carpenter drew up a petition and asked all the members of the congregation to sign it on leaving church on Sunday morning. The motion to restrain the activities of the mission was defeated and Seven Trees became the home of the first wave of bewildered children from Prague.

The accommodation issue immediately became a further problem. Fortuitously, another large house in the road became empty. This was the former home of Sir John Lubbock, Lammas, from which St Hugh's Prep School for Boys had just been evacuated. There was a gymnasium; an annexe for staff bedrooms; nurseries; and a garden with a bungalow for a resident gardener. In the main house there were very large rooms and 'adequate bathrooms'.

Once again the Mission had to face the opposition of neighbours and some of the council. The leader advised a petition to canvass the neighbours. There was a real triumph when 'the old gentleman who had been our most bitter opponent had since been largely won over. Though openly disliking children, he personally told me that our boys were the best behaved he had ever met and, rather rashly perhaps, added that if he could ever help me at any time he would be pleased to do so.' He was the first to sign the new petition and the refugee boys were able to move into what became known as Mount Zion.

One of the refugee children, Anna Meyer, now in her seventies recalls:

Both children's homes were staffed by women and a few men, who worked there for the love of God and, presumably, children too, plus their bread and board and quite modest pocket money. We called the senior one, a buxom lady with a fine singing voice, 'Mother', but having left my own mother behind it took me a while to call her that. The other staff were 'aunties', but there were no 'uncles' at Mount Zion.

A lifetime later in 1989 we had a happy, if nostalgic, reunion in Seven Trees; some of the 'kids' coming from overseas; some bringing husbands or wives and even grown-up children. As far as I know none of us had a criminal record, none had become a millionaire, but all appeared to be living relatively comfortably. Most had made a positive contribution to the country that took them in.

It seemed fitting to commemorate the Davidsons and the friends of the BMJ in a tangible way so we had a dedicated bench placed at the junction of Lubbock Road and Old Hill and bought a piano for a North London school for disabled children.

Michael Ferriss DFC, 1 August 1917–16 August 1940

One of Churchill's Few

Henry Michael Ferriss was born in London and was educated at St Joseph's, Blackheath and Stoneyhurst College before attending London University in 1935. He learned to fly with the University Air Squadron and also studied as a medical student at St Thomas' Hospital. In July 1937 he joined the RAF. After completing the course Ferriss was posted to No. 111 Squadron where he began to fly Hawker Hurricanes.

On 8 April 1940, Ferriss was flying when he shared in the probable destruction of a Heinkel 111 after firing a succession of short bursts at the enemy bomber and two days later he shared another 'kill'. When the intense fighting between the RAF and the Luftwaffe broke out in May, Ferriss was actively involved in flying daily patrols with the squadron in hostile skies. On Saturday 18 May en route to Valenciennes they encountered nine Bf 110s. Ferriss attacked a plane hitting the port engine and the enemy plane dived out of control with smoke pouring from its damaged engine. He engaged another plane and reported that he saw pieces break away from one engine before it issued volumes of black smoke.

The next day Ferriss was again in combat.

On the evening of 31 May, he was flying north of Dunkirk. Enemy fighters were sighted 600 metres above the Squadron which was patrolling at 5,000 metres. He reported that he had fired 1,840 rounds from his guns during the patrol.

On 6 June, Ferriss claimed two Bf 109s shot down and was awarded a DFC for his success. The *London Gazette* commented, 'During two consecutive days in May, Flying Officer Ferriss shot down a total of four Messerschmitt 110s although heavily outnumbered. Later, he shot down a further three Messerschmitt 109s. In these combats he has displayed outstanding ability.'

On 10 July 1940, the opening day of the Battle of Britain, Ferriss was on afternoon patrol. He shared in the destruction of enemy aircraft with other members of his squadron and then shot down a plane off Folkestone. His own aircraft was damaged. He managed to evade his attackers and got back to Croydon, where, despite a splinter in his leg, he climbed into a different Hurricane and took off again to join the fight.

On 28 July, Ferriss attacked and damaged a He59, 10 miles west of Boulogne. On 13 August, he shot down a Dornier 17 and damaged another. Two days later he claimed another Dornier. At 12.45 hours on 16 August, Ferriss attacked a formation of Dornier 17s in a head-on attack over Marden but he collided with one of the enemy bombers. He was killed and his Hurricane crashed over Paddock Wood.

Flight Lieutenant Henry Michael Ferriss DFC, the son of Henry and Violet Ferriss, who lived in Petts Wood, is buried in St Mary's churchyard, a brave pilot who demonstrated great ability and fighting spirit in combat. One of the many young men who fought in the skies during the Second World War and who earned the respect of Winston Churchill, 'Never, in the field of human conflict, was so much owed by so many to so few.'

The grave of Flight-Lieutentant
Michael Ferris.

The Cold War

The Edgebury bunker

During the Cold War of the 1950s and 60s, a network of civil defence underground
bunkers and hundreds of observation posts, located on high ground and manned by
The Royal Observer Corps supported by volunteers, were built. Their role, in the event
of conflict, was to become the eyes and ears of the RAF, responsible for identifying and
locating any bomb bursts, and tracking the subsequent and deadly radioactive fallout.

There was a subterranean bunker on the Edgebury Estate located on what is now a
horses' field beside Slades Drive. Communications between bunkers and observation posts
was by telephone lines; these were something of a giveaway to its location. The bunker
consisted of a 5 metre entrance shaft which accessed two rooms; one contained a chemical
toilet and a large monitoring room which was furnished with chairs; a table; shelves; a
cupboard and a pair of metal framed bunk beds. A ventilation shaft with two louvered
vents was located alongside the entrance shaft with a second shaft at the other end of the
room. Lighting was provided by a 12 volt battery behind the monitoring room door.

Edgebury fields above the Cold War bunker.

Opening in May 1965, it had a short life, closing in October 1968. The government decided the threat of nuclear attack had lessened and as part of massive cuts home defence services were reduced. The bunker is certainly no longer operational, all signs on the surface have been removed but some of what lay underneath remains, a secret under the horses' hooves.

8. Country Estates

Camden Park

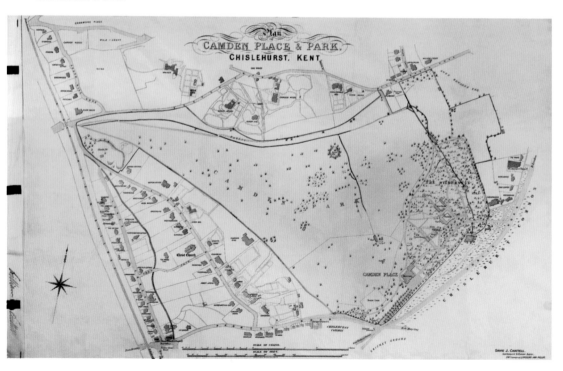

In 1860, a large area of Chislehurst was owned by Nathaniel John William Strode, having purchased the Camden Park Estate. He allowed a 'sham fight' to be conducted on the slopes of the park and people came in their thousands to view the extravaganza on 18 July 1860. The rationale behind it was to publicise the area for development. Members of Chislehurst Golf Club can see the plan of the event hanging on the walls of Camden Place.

Chislehurst was deemed to be a healthy place to live, green countryside away from the smog of central London, yet close enough to the city to be accessed by the railway which arrived in 1865.

There was a well in the grounds of the park that is now covered with a temple, which is a replica of the Monument of Lysicrates, the original of which stood on the slopes of the Acropolis in Athens for nearly 2,500 years. This forms the emblem of Chislehurst Golf Club which now owns Camden Place.

Yester Park

Strode sold off or leased many plots of land on the estate and country homes for the gentry and wealthy Victorian merchants were built. One such gentleman was Lord Arthur Hay, who became Viscount Walden in 1862 and then Marquis of Tweeddale in 1876. He lived on a 4 acre plot leased from Strode. He had been born just outside Edinburgh in the village of Yester. He named his house Walden Cottage and his butler witnessed the signing of the lease!

'Walden', as he styled himself, was President of the Zoological Society of London and a very keen ornithologist. He died in 1878 and his elaborately railed grave lies in St Nicholas churchyard. All that remains of the estate today is the gatehouse lodge to Yester Park.

Chislehurst golf club 'temple'.

Yester Park gatehouse lodge.

Camden Wood/Livingstone House

Off Willow Grove, part of the original Camden Park Estate, in the road, Beechcroft, is a grand Victorian house. Now called Livingstone House, this mansion was originally called Camden Wood. It dates back to 1869 and like Yester Park; Camden Wood had its own lodge, now a private dwelling.

From 1870 the house was owned by James Englebert Vanner, a dealer in silk and a prominent Methodist who had largely funded the Methodist Church along with his brother in law, George Hayter Chubb, of lock-and-safe fame and fortune. Vanner employed George Watto as a gardener at the house; this could be the link to the current name. One can see the south-facing loggia along the ground floor and the elaborate stone carvings around the front door.

Livingstone House is now a conference centre owned by the Unification Church. Along the fringes of the Camden Park Estate, it is possible to trace other former large houses by the remaining lodges: Greatwood and Oakwood on Yester Road; Walden Manor (originally Waratah) now the site of Kings Quarter; Elmstead Glade on Walden Road and Cranmore on Elmstead Lane. On the other side of the Commons on Old Perry Street (named after old pear orchards in the area) are the east and west lodges to the old estate of Homewood.

William Camden, a noted historian, came to escape the London air and made his home in Chislehurst in 1609. In 1760 ambitious lawyer, Charles Pratt, then Attorney General purchased Camden's house as his country estate. He was created a baron in 1765 and took the title Lord Camden. In 1791 he had 1,400 houses built on his lands in North London and gave the area the name of Camden Town.

Livingstone House, formerly Beechcroft.

East and West Lodge, Old Perry Street.

Chislehurst and St Paul's Cray Commons

These are lands that belong to all of us. The Commons exist today because they have never been built on nor used for agriculture given their poor quality soil. However, bearing in mind the derivation of the name Chislehurst, 'the gravelly clearing in the woods', the current ponds and various depressions in the land are reminders of the fact that they were formerly sources of gravel. With the arrival of the railway in 1865 and the development of housing on the edge of the Commons, there were concerns that the status of the Commons as open land was under threat.

The Sydneys of Frognal were the Lords of the Manor and increasingly exploiting the land around their estate. With increasing industrialization and suburbanisation of the country the Metropolitan Commons Act was passed in 1866 to prevent enclosure of common land and create schemes of management to preserve them. Here, a group of prominent local residents formed the Chislehurst and St Paul's Cray Commons Preservation Society which enshrined in law a Supplemental Act in 1888 which applied locally.

The commons are no secret to dog walkers and birdwatchers alike. We are lucky to have such green surroundings to the village. Ecologically diverse, they are forever protected by the Trustees of the Commons.

One former Chairman of the Conservators from 1941–1966, Clifford Platt, and also Chairman of Petts Wood Management Committee for thirty-five years, was awarded the MBE for his voluntary services to open spaces. There is a charming bench dedicated to his memory on Church Row facing the Commons which declares him, quite rightly, to be a 'defender of open space' (see opposite).

Memorial bench dedicated to Clifford Platt.

What is more secret (and should not be) is the amount of hard work that goes in to managing the land and the village ponds. Based at the Old Fire Station in Hawkwood Lane, there are two paid members of staff looking after 71.8 hectares of land supported by volunteers from the Friends of the Commons.

Hawkwood

At the end of Hawkwood Lane stood an eighteenth-century mansion, demolished in 1960. Vestiges of the estate remain in the form of gate posts and the avenue of tall lime trees near Garden Cottage. An overgrown ornamental lily pond can still be found in the National Trust owned Pond Wood.

A couple of buildings just out of sight beside the modern Hawk's Wing are a delightful secret. These are the Old Laundry, converted and civic design awarded in 1986 and The Old Stables. The latter is the weekly meeting place of the 5th Chislehurst Scouts.

In 1927, Colonel Francis Edlmann, then owner of Hawkwood purchased a further 47 acres of woodland, west of Willett Wood. When he died in 1950, all 168 acres of the estate were put on the market.

The subsequent owners of Hawkwood, Robert and Francesca Hall, also purchased the meadow in Watts Lane. They announced publicly in October 1957 that they would be bequeathing the estate to the National Trust but, tragically, Robert was killed in a car crash on Old Hill the following year. The donors may be somewhat unknown today but the view they protected is a joy for all to see.

Above: Hawkwood stables. *Below*: The view from Watts Lane – National Trust land.

The Edlmann stone in what became the Edlmann Memorial Wood is a dedication to the previous owner. On the reverse of the stone is a reminder of the sterling work of National Trust Committee Chairman, Clifford Platt.

The two estates of Camden Park and Hawkwood are linked by the Kyd Brook that runs through them both. The brook rises from two sources in nearby Farnborough, and a long stretch is visible in Hawkwood. It runs through the National Trust land, emerging below The Bickley public house, runs alongside Lower Camden and the lower part of Sundridge Avenue before heading into Sundridge Park. It flows to Kidbrook at Lewisham and eventually joins the River Ravensbourne and is then known as the Quaggy. In 1968 and 1977 the water levels rose to alarming levels, residents at the Yester Road end of Lubbock Road being rescued from their homes by boat. Flood defence systems are now in place and low-lying houses in the area receive telephone warnings from the Environment Agency at times of heavy rainfall.

Scadbury

Scadbury Park, to the west of Chislehurst, is a large area of land which preserves the bulk of the former Scadbury Manor. At the heart of the park is the site of the manor-house itself. It seems likely that a timber-framed house had been constructed by around 1200, and a moat dug around it.

The de Scathebury family became the richest family in Chislehurst parish, and were the Lords of the Manor until around 1347, when they disappear from documentary records. The subsequent ownership is not entirely clear until a wealthy London merchant, Thomas Walsingham, purchased the estate in 1424. The Walsinghams were to remain there for over 200 years, adding land in St Paul's Cray and Chislehurst to the core Scadbury estate. They remodelled the manor house partially or wholly in brick and a walled garden with brick archway were probably also constructed during this period.

The Walsinghams were also instrumental in rebuilding St Nicholas parish church, Sir Thomas Walsingham IV became Lord of the Manor of Chislehurst as well as Scadbury and is represented on the Chislehurst village sign in Royal Parade. This was unveiled on Coronation Day, June 1953, showing Sir Thomas being knighted by Queen Elizabeth I on her visit in 1597. The flint plinth to the timber column of the sign incorporates three old bricks from Scadbury Manor.

The Walsinghams sold the estate to Sir Richard Bettenson in March 1660 with Sir Edward Bettenson (1676–1733) becoming Lord of the Manor at the age of three; he was the last owner to live in the moated manor house. The manor house on the island was by that time a large brick and timber building. An inventory of 1727 lists some of the

Chislehurst village sign at Royal Parade.

rooms: Great Gate; Great Hall; kitchens; pantries and cellars. There were eight principal bedrooms, one described as Queen Elizabeth's Room above the Great Parlour. The corbels supporting the bridge across the moat can still be seen today.

As a young man Edward became addicted to gambling and was forced to sell the oak trees at Scadbury to pay his debts, timber being in great demand for housing and shipbuilding at the time.

In May 1734, an estate map shows that as part of the tenanted Scadbury Manor Farm, a farmhouse stood just outside the moat. This had originally been the manor's gate house. The farmhouse was extended over time to become a large Victorian mansion, known as Scadbury Park. After Edward's death, an August 1734 valuation of the estate describes the house '... being a large old timber building of no value more than as old materials'.

The estate passed to John Selwyn, nephew of Edward Bettenson, in May 1736, and given the state of disrepair he was never in residence during his six years of ownership and the manor house on the moated island was pulled down in 1738.

The manors of Chislehurst and Scadbury were then transferred to Thomas Townshend in December 1742 (his son, Thomas Townshend the second, became Lord Sydney in 1783) the family acquired the neighbouring Frognal Estate in 1749 and were resident there. In 1778 it was stated by the historian, Hasted, that 'the ancient mansion of Scadbury has been many years in ruins and there remains now only a farmhouse, built out of part of them.'

Around 1870 a Victorian house, Scadbury Park mansion was constructed on the site of the old farmhouse adjacent to the moat. By the later part of the nineteenth century Scadbury Park had become a large country house.

Remains of Scadbury motted manor.

After the death of the third and last Lord Sydney in 1890, the estate passed to the Hon Robert Marsham in 1893, who, in order to inherit, had to change his name to Marsham-Townshend and lived at Frognal until 1914. The Scadbury and Frognal estates were put up for sale in 1915. They did not sell, but Frognal was acquired by the War Office and became The Queen's Hospital in 1917, now Queen Mary's.

In 1896 five cottages were built on Perry Street and in 1904 another four cottages were built just north of the moat for estate workers; Archway Cottages were built in 1928 at the entrance to the estate from the Sidcup bypass.

Robert's son, Hugh, and grandson John, lived at Scadbury Park mansion from 1904 to 1975 except during the First World War when they lived at their London address.

In the early 1920s the Scadbury estate was developed as a commercial orchard and an apple store was built on the island. Between 1925 and 1930 Hugh Marsham-Townshend conducted excavations on the island and re-excavated the moat. The estate barn was hit by a V1 flying bomb in March 1945.

Hugh died in 1967 and John died in 1975. Following the death of John Marsham-Townshend, the last resident owner of the estate, who is buried in St Nicholas churchyard, the estate passed to his nieces. Scadbury Park mansion was completely destroyed by fire in January 1976.

The Scadbury estate was purchased by Bromley Council in 1983 and is now a nature reserve. The bluebells that carpet the ground every spring are not to be missed. The title

Lord of the Manor, which still has some legal functions, is now held by the eldest niece who is married to a Russian aristocrat.

Very little remains of the manor-house; foundations of the Walsingham brick house survive, but the only complete structure on the island today is the early twentieth century building once used as an apple store.

The manor site is open to the public annually each September and is carefully protected by volunteers of the Orpington and District Archaeological Society. In 2013 it was designated a scheduled monument by English Heritage and was added to the at risk register the following year. Archaeological digs at Scadbury have uncovered interesting items, including a rare Tudor sundial which is now part of the Bromley Museum collection.

We cannot leave Scadbury without exploring something of its potential to have irrevocably changed the story of Chislehurst. Thomas Walsingham IV and Christopher Marlowe were thought to be involved in the secret service founded by Sir Francis Walsingham, known as Queen Elizabeth I's 'spymaster', perhaps as couriers bringing information to her.

Marlowe was a great poet and playwright; he sometimes visited his patron Thomas Walsingham at Scadbury. In 1952 North American theatre critic, Calvin Hoffman, visited Scadbury looking for evidence of Marlowe. He made a further visit in 1956 to search for a chest in St Nicholas church that he thought contained evidence of plays written by Marlowe and now attributed to Shakespeare. The Walsingham Tomb in the Scadbury Chapel at St Nicholas church was opened at the request of Hoffman.

Opening the Walsingham Tomb.

However, all that was found was sand. This did not deter Hoffman from opening one of the two vaults beneath the floor in a further search thirty years later, but only stacked coffins were found and the search was abandoned.

Avalon/Black Mount

Avalon, off Summer Hill, was built for Scotsman, James Bruce in 1872 and originally called Black Mount. The daughter of James Bruce became involved with the gardener, eloped and married him and was subsequently never spoken to by her family again.

Richard Harding Butler was the next owner in 1905 and set about renovating the property and renamed it Avalon. He was the grandson of Joseph Harding, the inventor of the Cheddar Cheese making process and Richard married into the Austin family also from Somerset. They became fabulously wealthy, emigrated to Australia and formed a continuing habit of naming their houses 'Avalon' after their Somerset roots.

There are two large stone eagles on the roof of Avalon and compared with those on the chapel roof at St Mary's church, which are an Imperial memorial, these are very different. It is likely that they are the heraldic emblems of James Bruce.

The house became an approved school for girls after the Second World War but is now used by the Salvation Army as a residence and training centre for its overseas missionaries.

Bibliography

100 Years in the Wilderness, Tim Green (1997)

A Life Worth Living, C. B. Fry (1939)

A Walk around Chislehurst, Bromley Borough Technical Services Department (1972)

Bilbroughs, James J. McGrane (1994)

Chislehurst Golf Club, W. M. Mitchell (1994)

Discover Chislehurst, Darrell Spurgeon with Roy Hopper (2007)

Edwardian Chislehurst, Memories of a Village Baker, Arthur Battle (1988)

For King and Country, Researched and Compiled by Yvonne Auld (2011)

Genuine Fake, a Biography of Alan Watts, Monica Furlong (1986)

Imperial Chislehurst, T. A. Bushell (1974)

In Trust for Chislehurst, Clifford L. Platt MBE MA (1995)

Janet Clayton, Michael Meekums and Steve Archer of the Orpington and District Archaeological Society

My War Diary, Ethel 1914–1918, Ethel M. Bilbrough in association with IWM (2014)

Richmal Crompton: the woman behind Just William, Mary Cadogan (1986)

The History of Chislehurst, E. A. Webb, G. W. Miller and J. Beckwith (1899)

The Roses of No Man's Land, Lyn Macdonald (1984)

The Story of Kemnal Road, Chislehurst, Collected and Edited by Tony Allen and Andrew Thomas (2011)

Also Available from Amberley Publishing

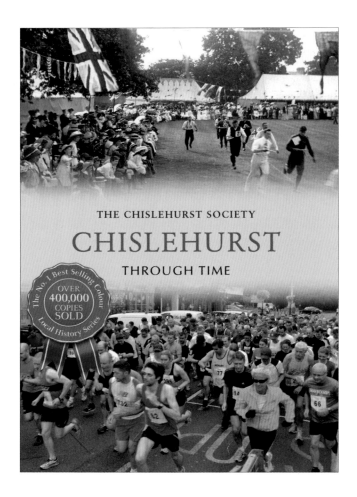

THE CHISLEHURST SOCIETY

CHISLEHURST

THROUGH TIME

The No. 1 Best Selling Colour Local History Series

OVER 400,000 COPIES SOLD

This fascinating selection of photographs traces some of the many ways in which Chislehurst has changed and developed over the last century.

978-1-4456-18395